Philip Carr-Gomm lives in Sussex, with his wife Stephanie and their children. A psychotherapist and the founder of the Lewes Montessori school, he began the study and practice of Druidism over thirty years ago, and for the last fifteen years has written, lectured, and held workshops and retreats on this spiritual tradition all over the world. He is author of *Druid Mysteries, The Druid Way*, and *Druidcraft*, co-author of *The Druid Animal Oracle* and *The DruidCraft Tarot*, and editor of *The Book of Druidry, The Rebirth of Druidry*, and *In the Grove of the Druids*. For more information see www.philipcarrgomm.druidry.org.

SERIES EDITOR: TONY MORRIS

Also available

What Do **DRUIDS** Believe?

Philip Carr-Gomm

GRANTA

Granta Publications, 12 Addison Avenue, London W11 4QR
First published in Great Britain by Granta Books 2006

Copyright © 2006, Philip Carr-Gomm

'Mind Games' written by John Lennon © 1973
Lenono Music, used with permission

Philip Carr-Gomm has asserted his moral right under the
Copyright, Designs and Patents Act, 1988, to be
identified as the author of this work.

All rights reserved. No reproduction, copy or transmissions
of this publication may be made without written
permission. No paragraph of this publication may be
reproduced, copied or transmitted save with written
permission or in accordance with the provisions of the
Copyright Act 1956 (as amended). Any person who does
any unauthorized act in relation to this publication may be
liable to criminal prosecution and civil claims for damages.

A CIP catalogue record for this book is available
from the British Library.

ISBN 978 1 86207 864 2

Typeset by M Rules
Printed and bound by CPI Group (UK) Ltd, Croydon, CR0 4YY

www.granta.com

*This book is dedicated
to the Mount Haemus Scholars —
that growing band of dedicated
souls who are determined to research,
articulate and understand Druidry.*

Contents

Acknowledgements

A maxim in creativity training is that you should ask very simple, apparently obvious questions to generate new insights and to deepen your understanding of a subject. I am very grateful to the series editor, Tony Morris, for inviting me to write this book, and for asking me to structure it around a series of very direct, simple questions. This helped me to think about a familiar subject with what is known in Zen Buddhism as 'Beginner's Mind', which made the experience of writing this book refreshing and illuminating. I would also like to thank Pamela Meekings-Stewart for providing the perfect retreat environment in New Zealand for working on the book, Ronald Hutton, John Michael Greer, Barbara Erskine, Sarah Fuhro and the many friends and members of the Order of Bards, Ovates and Druids who helped with their comments, encouragement and suggestions.

1

Druids in the Twenty-First Century – Who Follows Druidism Today?

What is Druidry? A Spiritual Path, a way of life, a philosophy, Druidry is all of these . . . Druidry today is alive and well, and has migrated around the world forming a wonderful web of people who honour and respect the Earth . . .

Cairistiona Worthington, *Druids – A Beginner's Guide*

A road protester who has chained himself to a tree to prevent it being torn down to build a motorway and the late Queen Mother entertaining guests at Clarence House might seem to have nothing in common. But an unusual thread connects them – as it connects characters as diverse as Winston Churchill and an expert forger, or the Archbishop of Canterbury and an advocate of free love and political revolution who ensured that cremation was legalized in Britain. This thread is Druidism.

Today probably about a quarter of a million people around the world are inspired by Druid ideas, but still the story of Druidism and of how it has evolved is little known outside its own community.

What exactly is a Druid? How do you become one, and what

does a practising Druid do? Is Druidism a religion, a cult, a New-Age fad? Is it based on fact or fantasy? Are those who follow Druidism as a spiritual way espousing a kind of pseudo-religion based on romantic notions of our past, or are they are actually on to something: practising a type of spirituality that is rooted in ancient heritage yet particularly suited to today's world?

Although I practise Druidry, I have tried to bring to this exploration as much objectivity and scepticism as I can muster. This has been possible, perhaps, because I dislike organized religion and rigid belief systems. The right to change one's opinions feels paramount, yet often religions seem to deny this, and as a result are sometimes capable of generating extraordinary intolerance, even cruelty. Although many of us feel a spiritual hunger, the challenge is surely to find a way to satisfy this hunger that frees us rather than traps us in dogma.

Druidism, or Druidry as it is often called, is remarkably free of dogma and is in many ways a very young movement, even though it bases itself on very old foundations. Some believe the term 'Druid' comes from the Celtic word for oak – *dru* – combined with the Indo-European root *wid* – to know – making the Druid a 'knower of the oak', in other words a 'forest sage'. Others believe the word comes from the pre-Indo-European roots *deru*, meaning 'strong', and *weid*, meaning 'to see', making a Druid a 'strong seer'.

Contemporary Druidry draws on a heritage of thousands of years, and yet many of its ideas and practices have only been formed over the last few hundred years. Unlike most of the established religions, which are based on doctrine formulated in the distant past, Druidry is developing its philosophy and practices in response to the spirit of the times. It is being shaped now rather than being preserved or simply passed on, and paradoxically, although it is inspired and informed by an ancient heritage, it is surprisingly free of the weight of the past. This leaves modern Druidry open to the criticism that it has been invented; but it also makes it a thoroughly contemporary spirituality that speaks directly to the needs of today.

Who Follows Druidism Today?

Twice a year, at the time of the solstices, the largest Druid group, the Order of Bards, Ovates and Druids, holds a big gathering in Glastonbury. Ceremonies are held on the Tor and at Stonehenge. There are talks and presentations, people eat, dance, sing and play music together. The two hundred or so participants include old and young people, men, women and children, some flamboyantly dressed, some in conventional clothes. You'd expect to see some behind a desk at an office, others at a pop festival. They come mainly from Britain and Ireland, but there are also people from America, Australia and all over Europe.

Druidism as a spiritual path appeals to all kinds of people, all over the world, because it directly concerns itself with the three most pressing problems of our age: the destruction of the environment, the alienation of the individual, and the commercialization and mass production of culture.

If you ask people why they are attracted to Druidism they will almost invariably offer as a first answer the fact that they love the natural world, and that they deplore the way in which they see it being exploited and damaged. They are looking for a spirituality that honours and works within Nature, rather than separately from it. They feel that modern living has separated us from the natural world and along with this sense of being separated from Mother Earth comes another sense of alienation: a feeling that we lead increasingly separate lives as political and economic pressures turn us from being citizens living in a community to being individual consumers.

As we lose touch with our sense of living within a community, and within the natural world, we are becoming increasingly isolated from our sources of spiritual sustenance. We may benefit materially from technology and globalization, but we will most likely exist in relationship to a series of boxes: waking up in a box, leaving it in a metal one to enter another made of glass and concrete, in which we will often stare into the little box of our computer before returning home in our metal box to relax in front of a television.

People drawn to Druidry want to break out of these boxes – to feel the land close to them and to feel part of a community of people with similar values and ideals. They are trying to undo the alienation of modern life by seeking their origins, both ancestral and spiritual, by exploring the past of their families and their culture, and by drawing on the inspiration of a tradition whose roots travel deep.

Every spiritual tradition was born within a particular culture. For Druidry this was Western Europe: mainland Britain, if we are to believe Caesar. But then, like seeds cast to the wind, traditions travel to distant lands to inspire people from other cultures. This has happened with Druidry, as it has with most religions and spiritual paths, so the fact that you call yourself Christian or Buddhist, for example, bears no relationship to your ethnic, geographical or cultural background. Similarly many people following Druidry have no Celtic ancestry, while others who do, often find in their Druidry a way of sensing a closer connection with their heritage.

The Appeal of Myth and Story

As well as being drawn to Druidry by a love of nature, or by wanting to get in touch with what they sense as their ancestral spirituality, many people are attracted to it because of their love of myth and storytelling. Just as modern society has separated us from the natural world, so it has also tended to separate us from meaningful art and story. Along with the movement towards individualistic consumerism has come the production of culture for the mass market. Some writers have seen in this process the attempt to create a 'McWorld' in which everything is seen through a Hollywood lens, which bleeds it of substance and meaning. Thankfully not everyone wants to live in McWorld, and there is a real thirst for art, films, stories and books which convey richer meanings and which are profound rather than superficial.

Druidry responds to this thirst by working with the power of stories and archetypal symbols. It explores old myths and legends, which may have originated in the teaching tales of the ancient Druids – told by the Bards of old, and transcribed in later times by Christian clerics. These tales resonate for many people, evoking ideas, images and feelings which help them feel closer to the realities of life.

Some people relate to Druidry simply as an interest, which they pursue like a hobby. They love the old tales, they like to visit ancient sites and to study history. Others might be members of Welsh, Cornish or Breton groups who attend ceremonies at the cultural events known as *Eisteddfodau*, which promote the arts, and enjoy the social, historical and cultural aspects of their activity. Others may be members of Druid fraternal or sororal organizations that are rather like Masonic groups. Or they may simply be investors in Druid Friendly Societies, which have evolved out of these organizations to offer insurance schemes and health-care plans.

In addition there are those who follow Druidry as a specifically spiritual way. They might call themselves Druids more or less from the start, or they might only do this when they have reached a specific level of training.

Accurate figures for the number of people interested in Druidism in its various manifestations do not exist, but there is enough information to make an estimate. Thousands attend the televised events in which the Druids of Wales appear each year at the Welsh National Eisteddfod, and hundreds attend similar events held in Cornwall and Brittany, while fraternal Druidism attracts about 11,000 people worldwide.[1] In 1996 a leading academic estimated that there were roughly 6,000 people practising Druidry as a spiritual way in Britain,[2] and a major study in 2001 in the USA estimated the figure there at 33,000.[3]

If we include the other countries of the world, this figure of 39,000 in Britain and the USA could be increased to a total of perhaps 45–50,000 people worldwide. Around such a group of people, who could be called 'Practising Druids', there is a much wider circle of those who are interested in the ideas of Druidry, and who incorporate some of these into their own personal brand of spiritual practice. Only a minority of the people who are inspired by Druidry actually join a Druid order or group. The majority, for reasons of time or inclination, are more likely to simply read books on the subject, informally celebrate the old festival times, and feel inspired by Druid lore. About 100,000 people in Britain[4] and around 426,000 people in the USA[5] regard themselves as Pagan. While not all these people will consider themselves inspired by Druidism, a good many will, and it is quite likely that the wider circle of influence beyond the dedicated followers of Druidism could well exceed a quarter of a million people worldwide.

Many of those drawn to Druidry consider themselves Pagan. They often actively dislike conventional religion, usually

Christianity, because of its doctrines or its historical record of intolerance and cruelty, and prefer instead the lack of dogma and the focus on the world of nature that Paganism offers. But there are others who find that studying Druidism helps them deepen their faith in another religion. The novelist Barbara Erskine writes of her experience:

When I was a child I set up an altar in woodland at the bottom of the garden. On it I put a little gold cross wedged into a lump of plasticine. Now, many years later, I realise this was a first expression of leanings towards what I now recognise as druidic Christianity, or Christian Druidism.

I came from a Church of England family and went to a school which worshipped daily in the chapel. Faith foundered however when I studied history at university. I encountered for the first time Christianity's downside: it had been too much mediated by politics, cruelty, misogyny and fundamentalism, caring little for Jesus's teachings of tolerance and love; it seemed to encourage exploitation of the natural world and it used the heavy hand of guilt rather than love to corral its followers. Like many others I questioned and fell away.

When I discovered Druidry it was a homecoming into a philosophy which encompassed all that I held dear and it brought me into the Western spiritual tradition, something which had been part of my soul without my realising it. My world was animistic. I had always prayed to the One God and all the gods, feeling that that expressed my true beliefs even though I was not comfortable with wholesale paganism. The last thing I expected was for my studies and meditations to illumine and rekindle my struggling Christian faith. Or that they would reconcile my certainties about a supernatural world of nature spirits, ghosts and energies which seemed to be unchristian, into a church which included angels and archangels and all the company of heaven.[6]

Druidism touches hearts and souls in different ways and it appeals to many people now because of its lack of exclusivity and uniformity. There are disagreements within the world of Druidry, as within any community, and there is no one universally accepted understanding of Druidism, but this has encouraged a diversity within the landscape of modern Druidry that is fertile and even exotic. How did it get to be this way? Where and when did Druidry begin?

2

How Did We Get Here?
The Origins of Modern Druidism

Any study of the druids must begin with a process of demysti-
fication . . .

Jean Markale, *The Druids – Celtic Priests of Nature*

Druidism is rooted in the culture and mythology of Western
Europe – in particular in those cultures which have come to be
known as Celtic, which stretch from Ireland and parts of
Portugal in the west to France, Switzerland and Austria in the
east. We first hear of it in the writings of Julius Caesar, who in
about 50 BCE wrote that Druidism originated in Britain.[7] But
some say that it originated elsewhere and much earlier, in Egypt
or India,[8] while mystics such as Dion Fortune and Rudolf
Steiner point, with clairvoyant rather than historical evidence,
to the even more mysterious land of Atlantis.

Whether Druidry's roots are indeed so exotic, or whether
the historical understanding that Druidism evolved in the
British Isles about 2,500 years ago is correct, the current revival
of interest in Druidism depends not so much upon the ancient
past as upon very recent history.

Modern Druidism, as it is practised by most Druids today, emerged out of two acts of rebellion that occurred virtually simultaneously on both sides of the Atlantic during that fertile and tumultuous period of the 1960s. In 1963 on the Carleton College campus in the USA a group called the Reformed Druids of North America was created as a humorous protest against mandatory Sunday morning chapel attendance, while the following year in England a historian, Ross Nichols, rebelled against the election of a new Druid Chief, and established his own group, the Order of Bards, Ovates and Druids.

Although both the RDNA and the OBOD were initially small groups, they exerted an influence over the coming years which resulted in Druidism finally emerging in the last decade of the twentieth century as a viable alternative to the more well-known and established spiritual paths.

Prior to the mid-1960s almost all Druid activity over the previous few hundred years had been confined to the cultural efforts of the Welsh Druids and the fraternal activities of the English Druids[9] – neither of which treated Druidry as a spiritual path in its own right. An exception could be found, however, in one type of Druidism that did focus on spiritual practice – even though it attracted only a handful of followers. At the dawn of the twentieth century a dynamic and vocal individual, George Watson MacGregor Reid, began promoting Druidism as a spiritual path that could unite followers of many faiths; the group that he led, the Universal Bond, became a vehicle for conveying many of the ideas that had been expressed by groups such as the Theosophical Society and the Order of the Golden Dawn in the previous century. Through the Universal Bond a complex tapestry began to be woven, which drew on the inspiration of the ancient Druids, the work of the Revival Druids of the previous three centuries, the teachings of the world religions, and the Western Mystery Tradition. The group held ceremonies at Stonehenge, campaigned for social justice, and promoted the Universalist Church, which later became incorporated into the Unitarian Church.

In the 1940s and '50s the Universal Bond, which had gradually evolved into being called the Ancient Druid Order, attracted to it two figures who would act as catalysts for the explosion of interest in Paganism that is occurring today: Gerald Gardner and Ross Nichols. Gardner became the seminal figure in the promotion of the religion of Wicca, or Pagan witchcraft, while Nichols developed Druidism by focusing its concerns on Celtic and British lore and mythology.[10] Nichols and many Wiccans were inspired by a book which has influenced much of the modern Pagan movement – Robert Graves' *The White Goddess*, which claimed to have discovered a Druidic calendar based on the trees and plants associated with 'Ogham', an alphabet of twenty-five strokes centred or branching off a single line that can be found inscribed on stones in Ireland dated to the fifth and sixth centuries. Both Nichols and Gardner came to adopt an eightfold cycle of observances which now lies at the heart of both Druid and Wiccan practices. In this cycle the observance of the solstices and equinoxes is combined with the celebration of the four traditional cross-quarter days around the first of February, May, August and November (see Chapter 8 for more details).

Gardner died in 1964 and so did the chief of the Ancient Druid Order – MacGregor Reid's son, Robert. A new chief was elected, but Nichols decided he wanted to work with Druidism in a different way, and formed his own order, which has since grown to become the largest Druid group in the world. While his group was formed out of a serious desire to deepen Druidism as a spiritual practice, the Reformed Druids of North

America were founded a year earlier partly as a prank to avoid church services, and partly as a protest against compulsory attendance. The initiative proved creative: since students who claimed they were Druids were obliged to hold alternative rites, they found themselves becoming seriously interested in new ways of worship – and Druidism. The writings and activities of the RDNA inspired the creation of the largest Druid group in America today, the ADF (A Druid Fellowship), out of which other groups have emerged to develop and enrich contemporary Druidism.

By 1969 Druids were starting to feature in the burgeoning counter-culture. John Lennon consciously or intuitively knew that Peace and Love, the cornerstones of counter-cultural idealism, were deeply connected with Druidism, and so he sang about this in his 'Mind Games':

> We're playing those mind games together,
> Pushing the barriers, planting seeds.
> Playing the mind guerrilla,
> Chanting the Mantra, 'Peace on Earth'.
> We all been playing those mind games forever
> Some kinda druid dudes lifting the veil.
> Doing the mind guerrilla,
> Some call it magic, the search for the grail.

In the same year that this song was released, a book about Stonehenge and the 'ley lines' which seemed to connect ancient sites across the British landscape appeared, which rapidly became a cult classic. *A View over Atlantis* by John Michell appealed to the baby-boom generation who were living through the era of 'Flower Power' and had become attracted to Eastern religions. Michell's book introduced them to their own exotic and mysterious heritage, and although *A View over Atlantis* was not directly about Druidism, Michell succeeded in educating the counter-culture in the power of this spiritual heritage that, just like the similar tradition of Hinduism at the other end of the Indo-European arc, seemed to speak directly to their spiritual needs.

Despite the popularity of Michell's book and a growing interest in the pre-Christian heritage of Britain and Ireland, with its sacred sites, and the mysterious lines of energy that were said to connect them, the practice of Druidry as a spiritual way was still confined to a handful of people: those members of the Ancient Druid Order founded by MacGregor Reid, and those of the Order of Bards, Ovates and Druids founded by Ross Nichols. It wasn't until the 1980s that this handful began to grow into the thousands of Druids who exist today.

As the popularity of alternative approaches to healing and spirituality, loosely termed 'New Age', grew during the decade or so after the appearance of *A View over Atlantis*, there developed a thirst for Celtic spirituality, stimulated to a great extent by two prolific writers: Caitlín and John Matthews. From the mid-eighties they began to mine, articulate and popularize the treasure trove of spiritual wisdom found in the old Welsh and Irish manuscripts, which, until then, had only been studied by academics. Druidism was often the subject of their researches, and their work provided much of the source material for numerous writers on Celtic mythology, the Grail, Druidry and Paganism, and succeeded in fuelling a widespread interest in Celtic spirituality in Britain and the United States.

By the eighties the time was ripe for a growth in the popularity of Druidism. The New Age was in full swing, the Church, and monotheistic religions in general, were seen by many people as increasingly part of the problem rather than part of the solution to the world's ills, and in addition there was now an intense awareness of the environmental disaster that threatened the planet. Even though Druidry had no practitioners who had inherited their traditions in an unbroken line from their ancestors, and even though it was no longer taught or practised in a tribal context, it still represented to many the indigenous pre-Christian spiritual and magical heritage of the far west of Europe – a territory that included Brittany, Ireland and the British Isles.

Once more, simultaneously on both sides of the Atlantic, Druidry took a leap forward in its development. In 1984 Isaac Bonewits founded the Druid group, ADF and I was asked to develop a course of teaching in Druidry.

Bonewits, the first American student to complete a university degree in Magic, five times married and an enthusiastic advocate of polyamory, had been a member of the RDNA and combined their ideas with his own researches to offer a Druidism that was distinctly religious – with a polytheistic theology and an emphasis on the importance of scholarship and the development of liturgy.

I had known and studied with Ross Nichols, had trained in psychology and psychotherapy, and in 1988 was asked to lead the Order he had founded twenty-four years previously. The Order published the course that I had created with the help of a number of writers, including Ross Nichols and John and Caitlín Matthews. Rather than presenting Druidry as a religion, the course offered a journey of spiritual and psychological exploration inspired by Druidry, and based upon the philosophy and the ideas that had become associated with it. The course seemed to answer a need, and by the close of the millennium four thousand people around the world were working with it. In the USA thousands had also become attracted to

Druidism through the work of the RDNA, ADF and other groups, and in doing this had begun to practise Druidism as a spiritual way. Soon after the twentieth century had opened, a handful of people had begun doing this. Now, as the century closed, thousands were. Helped by two impulses of renewal and change, in the 1960s and the 1980s, Druidism was now more popular than it ever had been. But it was not the thoroughly modern creation it appeared to be at first sight. Its rebirth in recent times was entirely dependent upon the past – and it developed out of a period of more than two centuries of scholarship and speculation.

3

The Roots of a Tradition

As we settle into this new century it is of vital importance that
we reconnect with our Druidic roots.

Tom Cowan, *Of Ancient Shapes and Memories*

In the late seventeenth century a complex of influences con-
verged to trigger an intense interest in the Druids that heralded
a period often called the 'Druid Revival', the most important
part of which occurred during the late eighteenth and early
nineteenth centuries. The modern Druid movement, which
started in the early twentieth century and gained momentum
in the 1960s, has grown out of this Revival period in both
senses of the term, having developed out of it, and in reaction
to it.

The Druid Revival began as the influence of the
Enlightenment encouraged enquiry and diminished the necessity to conform with Church doctrines. As the classical texts
describing ancient Druids became more readily available in
translation through the development of printing, scholars in
Britain, France and Germany became fascinated with the Greek
and Roman accounts of their pre-Christian ancestors.

Two of the most significant of these accounts, written by Julius Caesar and Diodorus Siculus, painted a picture of the Druids as scholars and religious leaders who functioned in a similar way to the priestly caste of the Hindu Brahmins: officiating at sacrifices, teaching philosophy and star lore, and conveying an oral tradition that required students to learn many verses by heart. Druids were exempt from military service and the taxes raised to pay for it. They advised chieftains and had a reputation for pacifying armies about to fight.

They described a darker side of Druidism, too, in which Druids were present at the sacrifice of criminals, or sometimes innocent people, who were burnt alive in wicker cages, or killed in the attempt to divine the future from their death throes. We cannot be sure that any of the classical authors were recounting the truth, but the description they have left us of wise sages calming warring tribes and teaching in forest groves has tended to endure over the image of their presiding over human sacrifice. Likewise, medieval Irish literature contains references to Druids as the wisest and most learned people of their time, who acted as advisors to local political leaders, and as wizards and magicians.

Inspired by these positive images of the ancient Druids, scholars in the seventeenth and eighteenth centuries saw them as 'noble savages' – an elite who were the guardians of an indigenous religion which was the precursor of Christianity. This perception was reinforced with reports of the noble savages living in America, who reminded Europeans of their Pagan forebears.

It wasn't long before the ancient guardians of the indigenous religion became associated with the many mysterious monuments which scattered the land. In the 1660s the versatile scholar, John Aubrey, suggested that the megalithic remains of

Britain had been built by the Druids, and intrigued by this, a man who was to become one the founding fathers of the modern science of archaeology, William Stukeley, visited Stonehenge in 1719. For the next five years he made annual visits to Wiltshire – carrying out a detailed study of both Stonehenge and Avebury. In his book *Stonehenge, a Temple Restored to the British Druids*, he popularized the notion that the Druids had built the most famous of stone circles, and that they were also responsible for the other megalithic monuments so well distributed throughout Britain.

The haunting presence of Stonehenge, and the classical texts describing the Druids, were inspiring, but the texts also reported disappointingly that the Druids conveyed an oral teaching, leaving eighteenth-century scholars impotent to explore in any detail their philosophy and practices. They combed both the classical sources and medieval Welsh and Irish literature for clear and extended statements of what the Druids had believed and taught, and found none. Into this vacuum stepped an extraordinary character: Edward Williams, who lived from 1747 to 1826 and took on the name of Iolo Morganwg. A stonemason and accomplished poet who played a significant role in promoting Unitarianism in Wales, Iolo set about constructing a body of lore that he then passed off as authentic ancient Druidism. His extensive knowledge of Welsh literary traditions, his theological explorations, and perhaps his use of laudanum, helped him to create a system that succeeded in providing much of the inspiration for the writing on Druidism into the modern era.

Woven into Iolo's work are strands of inspiration drawn from his knowledge of Welsh folklore and literature, and his visits to many of the old houses and libraries of Wales. It took nearly a hundred years for academics to prove that he had fabricated his material, and even though no expert in Welsh literature now believes that Iolo drew on any pre-existing tradition, an increasing number are coming to respect and celebrate him as an original genius. He is now seen both as a literary fraudster and as a social reformer with a positive legacy that continues to this day.

The Eisteddfod movement only experienced a revival and grew to become a major feature of Welsh culture once it had adopted Iolo's Druidic institution, which he called 'The Gorsedd'. He introduced the idea of the Gorsedd in 1792, when he led an Eisteddfod on London's Primrose Hill, and it was adopted by the Welsh Eisteddfod in 1819. The Eisteddfod, as a cultural phenomenon, has genuine roots in the ancient past of the Celts and Druids, whereas the Gorsedd is Iolo's invention. Its honorary members include the Archbishop of Canterbury and the late Queen Mother. Every school in Wales now holds an annual Eisteddfod, and the national event acts as a focus and stimulus to a broad range of cultural and literary initiatives. Once the Eisteddfod movement had adopted the ritual and institution of the Gorsedd, its influence extended to Brittany and Cornwall. In a time when their languages and culture had become marginalized, Iolo Morganwg's Druidism restored a pride in their heritage to the Bretons, Cornish and Welsh.

Just over a decade before Iolo's introduction of the Gorsedd in 1792, a Druid organization had already been created, but it was a distinctly different phenomenon: its purposes were social and fraternal rather than cultural. The Ancient Order of Druids, founded by a man named Hurle in 1781 in a pub in London's Poland Street, was formed to provide mutual support for members – modelling itself along the lines of Freemasonry. It offered social gatherings, and a type of ceremonial similar to those of fraternal societies, where a Bible was placed on the lectern at each meeting, and discussion of religion prohibited.

Most lodges were open only to males, though some 'Ladies' Lodges' were opened.

These lodges proliferated throughout England, and then abroad in most corners of the British Empire and in parts of Europe. In 1908 the young Winston Churchill was initiated into the Order, and by 1933 the Order had over a million and a half members.[11] The lodges produced engraved certificates, rings and even porcelain tea sets, which are sometimes discovered in antique shops or are unearthed as ancestral heirlooms, with families remembering that 'Granddad was a Druid'. But even though the Druid was used as a symbol of the wise philosopher, most members of the Ancient Order of Druids, like most members of the Gorsedd, considered themselves Christian, and the Order's main purposes were charitable and social.

Over the years a number of schisms occurred, resulting in different groups forming, some of which became Friendly Societies that offered members savings schemes and insurance policies. The Druids Friendly Society in Australia flourishes to this day and has an impressive website (www.druids.com.au). Some of these groups are affiliated to the 'International Grand Lodge of Druidism' (www.igld.org) which holds congresses and unites groups in over a dozen countries.[12]

Some Freemasons also formed fraternal Druid groups during the nineteenth century, the most famous being the Ancient and Archaeological Order of Druids, formed in 1874 to study the connections between Freemasonry and the Druid tradition. In the days before the introduction of the National Health Service, and before adequate insurance cover, a tragedy of illness or bereavement often resulted in families falling into poverty. The fraternal movement gave financial aid to members' families who were struck by illness or loss, and their development in some cases into Friendly Societies was a natural outcome of this function.

Although fraternal Druidry adopted some of Iolo's material, his legacy only becomes problematic when we consider the third type of Druid movement, which relates to Druidry not as an inspiration for cultural or fraternal activities, but as a spiritual path in its own right. This movement, starting in the early twentieth century, also drew upon Iolo's writings – in particular his 'Druid's Prayer', his Gorsedd ritual, and some of his cosmology.

THE GORSEDD/DRUID'S PRAYER

Grant, 0 God, Thy protection;
And in protection, strength;
And in strength, understanding;
And in understanding, knowledge;
And in knowledge, the knowledge of justice;
And in the knowledge of justice, the love of it;
And in that love, the love of all existences,
And in the love of all existences, the love of God,
and all goodness.

Iolo Morganwg claimed that this prayer was composed by Talhaearn, the first Welsh poet known to history. Morganwg wrote several different drafts of it, of which this was the one generally adopted after his death.

Cultural Druids, such as the Archbishop of Canterbury, have found little problem in reciting Iolo's Druid's Prayer while participating in a ritual that uses some or all of his material.[13]

Many spiritual Druids also use Iolo's prayer, though they often address it to the 'Goddess' or 'Gods' or 'Spirit' rather than 'God', depending upon their beliefs about the nature of Deity, and they will often use elements of his ritual to open their own meetings.

But not everyone is happy with this use of Iolo's material. In Britain and France, much of Druidry as a spiritual path has evolved as a result of Iolo's influence, and many groups continue to use at least some of his material, while recognizing its history – justifying its use on the pragmatic grounds that it has been in use for two hundred years and has, in this sense, become traditional. But in the USA the tendency has been to reject Iolo's work entirely, although several Druid groups there – notably the Ancient Order of Druids in America – consider Iolo's creations an important part of the modern Druid tradition and use them as such.

Iolo fabricated a body of lore in an attempt to fulfil a desire amongst his contemporaries to learn about the philosophy and ideals of the ancient Druids. The classical authors had written enough about these figures to inspire readers, but had failed to offer more than a brief glimpse into their world. The era of Druidry that they described lasted about a thousand years – from perhaps 400 BCE to 600 CE. But by the sixth century all of Europe was Christian, and overt Pagan practice had all but ceased to exist. Iolo and his contemporaries were separated by over a thousand years from the world of the ancient Druids. He attempted to span this gap in time with his imagination, and perhaps with scraps of genuine lore, but ironically, as Iolo set about his task, a movement was just beginning which would in the end fulfil the yearning for a sense of what genuine Druid lore might have been in a much more satisfying way.

Gradually, from the mid-nineteenth century onwards, scholars began to study folklore and there was a revival of interest in Celtic literature, initiating a period known as 'The Celtic Twilight', which was stimulated to a great extent by writers such as W. B. Yeats, George Russell and Fiona Macleod. The disciplines of Anthropology, Folklore Studies, Archaeology and History all began to take an interest in the pre-Christian past. Celtic Studies were born as an academic discipline and Celtic mythology and literature began to be researched in earnest.[14]

Some of the material being unearthed and discussed in academic and literary circles was eagerly studied in the twentieth century by the new disciplines of archetypal psychology and mythic studies, but surprisingly, it took until the 1960s for the Druid movement to take notice of these developments. Cultural Druids really needed only the pomp and ceremony of Iolo's Druidism to provide an impressive setting for their Eisteddfodau. Fraternal Druids were never seriously engaged in research into Druidism, since their purpose lay in social and charitable work, and the spiritual Druids had evolved such a satisfying body of teachings that few of them looked elsewhere for enlightenment.

It required a new impulse for spiritual Druidry to start taking on board, in any quantity, material which would free it of the stigma of being an invented tradition based upon a literary fraud. When Ross Nichols broke with the Ancient Druid Order to found the Order of Bards, Ovates and Druids, he prioritized the process of focusing on historical and Celtic material. Morganwg's contributions played a diminishing role in this new Druidism, until by the beginning of the twenty-first century it was confined to the use of his Druid's Prayer, and a few elements of ritual and lore. In the USA no such break with the recent past was needed, and modern Druidry there began the process of assimilating much of the latest findings in academic research.

After two centuries of an ambivalent history, Druidism has finally emerged over the last forty years to offer a spiritual way that genuinely draws on an ancient heritage for inspiration, while making no claim to be identical to the Druidism that was practised two thousand years ago.

4

Significant Druids –
Key Figures from the Past

Although the Druids have left no certain, visible monuments of their religion, they appear to have left enduring memorials in the minds of men.

F. E. Halliday, *A History of Cornwall*

Although modern Druidry as a spiritual practice has only evolved recently, it draws on a heritage that stretches far back in time, and we can read a number of accounts of prominent Druids from the ancient past which have profoundly influenced our perception of Druidism today. Just as accounts of early Christian saints, Tibetan lamas, or Indian gurus blend fact and legend, so too with these figures we cannot be sure where historical accuracy gives way to mythic vision. Nevertheless the stories of their lives can inspire followers of Druidism.

There is a common misconception that the ancient Druids were a male priesthood. This almost certainly isn't correct. Female Druids (*bandrui*) are mentioned in the old Irish texts, and it was said that the famous figure of Irish legend Fionn

MacCumhaill (Finn MacCool) was raised by a female Druid, while king Conchobar's mother was a Druid called Nessa.

Gaine daughter of pure Gumor
Nurse of mead-loving Mide,
Surpassed all women though she was silent;
She was learned and a seer and a Druid.
                    The Metrical Dindsenchas, Ireland

The classical authors also mention Druidesses. Dio Cassius writes of one named Ganna who went on an embassy to Rome and was received by Domitian, son of Emperor Vespasian. Pomponius Mela mentions nine virgin priestesses, who seem to be Druids, who lived on the island of Sena, in Brittany, and were able to predict the future. Aelius Lampridius, writing in the fifth century CE, mentions a Druidess foretelling the defeat of Alexander Severus: 'Go forth but hope not for victory,' she counselled, 'nor put your trust in your warriors.'[15]

The most famous woman to have espoused Druidry is perhaps Boudicca (sometimes known as Boadicea) who, as leader of the Iceni tribe, was almost certainly steeped in Druidism. In 60 CE she led a revolt against the Romans which nearly succeeded in ousting them from Britain. Because she would not yield to the command of the local Roman governor, she was flogged and her daughters were raped. In fury she raised an army which sacked the Roman towns of London, Colchester and St. Albans. The cities were burnt to the ground and thousands were killed.

The classical writer, Dion, in an imaginative account, described how she used a hare to divine the outcome of her first battle: 'When she had finished speaking to her people, she employed a species of divination, letting a hare escape from the fold of her dress; and since it ran on what they considered the auspicious side, the whole multitude shouted with pleasure, and Boadicea, raising her hand toward heaven, said, "I thank thee, Andraste [goddess of battle and victory] . . . I supplicate and pray thee for victory."'

But in the end Boudicca was defeated by the Romans, and rather than suffer at their hands she committed suicide by drinking from a poisoned chalice.

Fidelma – the Irish Druid

In the most famous epic in Irish mythology, the *Tain Bo Cuailnge*, the Cattle Raid of Cooley, we learn of another powerful female Druid, Fidelma. Queen Medb of Connacht is about to engage her armies in battle with King Conchobar of Ulster. She consults Fidelma, who tells her that she has just returned from 'learning verse and vision in Albion'. Medb asks her if she possesses the Light of Foresight – in other words, whether she can see into the future. Fidelma confirms that she is indeed a seer, and foretells defeat for Queen Medb.

This is how Fidelma is described: 'She had yellow hair. She wore a speckled cloak fastened around her with a gold pin, a red embroidered hooded tunic and sandals with gold clasps. Her brow was broad, her jaw narrow, her two eyebrows pitch black, with delicate dark lashes casting shadows halfway down her cheeks. You would think her lips were inset with Parthian scarlet. Her teeth were like an array of jewels between the lips. She had hair in three tresses; two wound upward on her head and the third hanging down her back, brushing her calves. She held a light gold weaving rod in her hand, with gold inlay. Her eyes had triple irises. Two black horses drew her chariot, and she was armed.'[16]

Male Druids are often equally formidable. They are inevitably cited in the old Irish texts as possessing magical powers, and when we read accounts of them we are propelled into a world reminiscent of *The Lord of the Rings*. The blind Mog Ruith, for instance, engages in a spectacular struggle against the opposing Druids of King Cormac. He is blind because he has lost one eye in the Alps, and the other by stopping the course of the sun for two days. He has a bird headdress and a wheel with oars, which he uses to fly through the sky. He hurls magic stones which turn into eels, and at one point takes slivers of wood from the spears of soldiers, mixes these with butter, and then hurls the resulting ball into a fire whilst chanting incantations for victory.

Behind the story we can discern the elements of modern Druidic practice. In Druidism today, the four elements of Earth, Air, Fire and Water are powerful symbols, and here the old Druid works with the powers of all four: Mog Ruith is a master of fire, knows how to use air with his magical 'druidic breath', he divines with samples of earth to choose land for himself, and is able to make water flow in times of drought.

The Greek geographer, Strabo, mentions a figure who later commentators have called a Druid – a man named Abaris who, like Mog Ruith, could fly through the sky. He is said to have visited Greece several times in around 770 BCE, transported by a golden arrow, and to have healed the sick, foretold the future, and worked miracles. Some have suggested that he symbolizes not a person but an ancient medical tradition, while writers in the Revival period believe that he might have been responsible for teaching Pythagoras the doctrines of the Druids. This neatly explains the classical authors' claims that the Druids taught Pythagoreanism: they were in fact teaching original Druidism, which the Pythagoreans had since adopted. Although historians give no credence to this claim, some commentators have reinforced this bold assertion by noting that some of the old stone monuments of Britain are built using Pythagorean geometry over 2,000 years before Pythagoras, suggesting a current of knowledge that could have passed from the pre- and proto-Druidic cultures of the British Isles to the classical culture of Greece.

The Roman writer, Cicero, mentions that he met a Gallic Druid, Divitiacus of the Aedui tribe. Divitiacus claimed to be learned in the ways of the natural world, and was able to make predictions from observing the flight of birds. Caesar also wrote about him, since he was an ally of Rome, but never referred to him as a Druid. As always with early accounts of Druids, we have frustratingly little material about these enigmatic figures, and yet details in many accounts, such as Cicero's, tally with what we know from other sources. The Celts' divination by bird flight (ornithomancy) was noted by Diodorus, and the Irish texts speak of the art of *Neldoracht*, or cloud-watching for portents. The movement of birds, the sky and the wind do indeed carry messages to us – if not of spirits, then of distant sounds, of changing weather, and with winds such as the Mistral in France or Fon in Switzerland even today, of alterations in pressure which lead to changing moods and the increased risk of depression and suicide.

In the accounts of notable Druids from the more recent past it is easier to separate fact from fancy, and in doing this appreciate their humanity as much as any specific contribution to Druidry they might have made. The characteristic they all share is one of daring to be different. Each in their own way was eccentric, and each has made an impact on the way Druidism is understood or practised today.

As we saw in the last chapter, in the mid-eighteenth century William Stukeley's book *Stonehenge, a Temple Restored to the British Druids* captured the public's attention and stimulated the Druid Revival which had already begun in the previous century.

Stukeley was fascinated by Pythagoreanism, Neo-Platonism and the Egyptian Mysteries, in addition to Druidism. His friends called him 'The Druid', and after he had met the Princess of Wales, he wrote to her as 'Veleda, Archdruidess of Kew'. He created a Druid temple in his garden – laying it out as a sacred landscape, with an apple tree covered with mistletoe at the centre of concentric circles of hazels and evergreens. Beside an altar he built a tumulus, and when his wife miscarried they ritually buried the foetus on the camomile lawn they had planted in front of the altar. After an earlier miscarriage, a friend had written to Stukeley urging him to 'assemble the sacred college of druids'. Unfortunately no further references to this mysterious group have been found.[17]

The revival of interest in the Druids encouraged by Stukeley received a complex boost to its development when *Barddas*, a collection of Iolo Morganwg's writings, was published in 1862.

In the 1890s, a courageous Welshman, Owen Morgan, Archdruid of a group founded in the tradition of Iolo Morganwg, issued *Light in Britannia*, an extraordinary book whose five subtitles reveal how daring it was to publish such a work in Victorian England: *The Mysteries of Ancient British Druidism Unveiled*; *The Original Source of Phallic Worship Revealed*; *The Secrets of the Court of King Arthur Revealed*; *The Creed of the Stone Age Restored*; *The Holy Grail Discovered in*

Wales. Morgan became the first writer to propose that Druidism was a duotheistic fertility religion, with one god comprising all other gods, and one goddess containing all other goddesses – a theory which has come to dominate the modern Pagan revival as the fundamental theology of Wicca, though not of contemporary Druidry, which embraces many theistic approaches.

Unbowed by the prevailing cultural climate, which must have received his ideas frostily to say the least, Morgan claimed that Jesus symbolized the creative power of deity and was thus a phallic symbol. Less controversial was the suggestion that he also symbolized the reborn sun of the winter solstice. Morgan felt he could trace the underlying sexual symbolism in religions, but far from subjecting these symbols to Freudian reductionism he took the approach familiar to alchemists, Taoists and Tantrics, and saw sexuality as sacred. For him, Pagan nature worship was the true religion, and Christianity was only valid because it unknowingly preserved the old fertility mysteries.

William Price was another great Welsh eccentric and equally undeterred by other peoples' prejudices or opinions. Born in 1800, Price experienced conflict with authority from an early age. His father's naked walks across the Welsh hillsides attracted the fury of the local churches, and when Price himself started campaigning for workers' rights he was obliged to flee to Paris for seven years. He clearly had a sense of humour, writing a thank-you letter to the British detectives who had been looking for him on the boat to France. He had disguised himself as a woman and they had courteously helped him on board.

When he returned to Wales he decided to call himself an Archdruid and practised as a healer, drawing on his medical training in London. He was vegetarian, refused to treat patients who smoked, and refused to wear socks on hygienic grounds. He advocated free love, and at the age of eighty settled down with a much younger woman. Three years later their son was born, but died in infancy. Price insisted on cremating him himself, and was arrested and jailed for this. His case was heard at the Cardiff Assizes in 1884, where the judge ruled that cremation was legal, as long as it was done without nuisance to others. In this way William Price, the Druid, became directly responsible for cremation being legalized in Britain, with the first officially sanctioned cremation being held a year later.

In 1913 a flamboyant character appeared on the public stage when he objected to being made to pay to worship at Stonehenge. A photograph of him confronting a policeman by the turnstile to the monument appeared in the *New Life* journal. George Watson MacGregor Reid had returned from America where, like William Price, he had been campaigning for workers' rights – this time in the New York docks. It was probably in New York that he became a minister of the Universalist Church and discovered Naturopathy (an alternative healing method using the powers of Nature). Now he was back in Britain where in the well-established tradition of Revival Druidry he began a long and varied career, becoming not only the leader of the Universal Bond which later became the Ancient Druid Order, but also minister of the Universalist Church in Clapham and a pioneer Labour Party campaigner. He published a magazine that combined radical politics with Druidism and Universalism, and that carried advertisements for Naturopathic products, such as dietary supplements. He championed the cause of the Senussi tribes people in the Libyan desert, then being attacked by the Italians, and supported a prophet known as the Bab, whose teachings inspired the Baha'i movement.

Later in his life MacGregor Reid started a Universalist and health retreat centre in Sussex, dying at the age of ninety-five with the distinction of apparently being the only person who had attempted election to both the House of Representatives in America and the Houses of Parliament in Britain.

MacGregor Reid's interest in health was echoed by a later Chief of the Ancient Druid Order, Thomas Maughan, who was a remarkable healer, largely responsible, along with a colleague, John Da Monte, for initiating the training of lay homoeopaths in England. Prior to their initiative only medical doctors could become practising homoeopaths.

Once Maughan became chief, a number of fellow Druids decided to form a new group and in 1964 the Order of Bards, Ovates and Druids was founded, led by Ross Nichols – a man who was to become one of the most influential figures in the modern Druid movement. Nichols read history at Cambridge. A published poet and journalist, at the age of thirty-eight he became the owner and principal of a private London college, which he directed until the end of his life. A dedicated naturist and vegetarian, when fifty-two he joined the Ancient Druid Order, and studied with it until becoming chief of his new Order a decade later. Stimulated by Robert Graves' exploration of bardic poetry in *The White Goddess*, and by his own researches into Celtic and British mythology, Nichols began to articulate a Druidry founded upon these sources of inspiration. His *Book of Druidry*, published after his death in 1990, helped the Order he founded become the largest Druid organization in the world.

The achievements of a notable male figure in any movement often depend upon the less publicized achievements and influence of a woman, and for Ross this was the gifted writer Vera Chapman, who helped him to found the Order and who provided him with the sort of peer support and intellectual stimulus that he needed. Born in 1898, she was one of the first women to matriculate as a full member of Oxford University. In her later years she achieved success as an author with a trilogy which focused on the role of women in the Arthurian tales. Recognizing the importance of J. R. R. Tolkien, she founded the Tolkien Society in 1969.

In looking back at the notable Druids of the last centuries we see a collection of individuals who share a common enthusiasm for exploring unconventional ideas. We might think that a spirituality needs a lineage of pious 'holy' men and women rather than the eccentrics and mavericks just described, but closer examination of the key figures in any spiritual tradition show that they, too, often rebelled against the status quo and refused to conform. They challenged conventional morality and behaviour, and proposed or invented new ways of being in the world. In the lineage of Druidry we find not saintly figures, but men and women who broke the mould: who dared to be different, while adhering to strong principles. They were often politically active – with many key figures from the Revival period onwards being interested in radical politics, supporting individual liberty and social justice. They were naturopaths, vegetarians, naturists or healers, poets, historians and philosophers. They were attracted to Druidism because their spirituality was founded in a passion for Nature and history, mythology and ancient monuments. And each – in their own way – can act as an inspiration for us if we, too, have such passions.

5

What Do Druids Believe?

Above all else, Druidry means following a spiritual path rooted in the green Earth. It means embracing an experiential approach to religious questions, one that abandons rigid belief systems in favour of inner development and individual contact with the realms of nature and spirit.

John Michael Greer, *The Druidry Handbook*

Life, Meaning and Purpose

One of the most striking characteristics of Druidism is the degree to which it is free of dogma and any fixed set of beliefs or practices. It honours the uniqueness of each individual's spiritual needs. In this way it manages to offer a spiritual path, and a way of being in the world that avoids many of the problems of intolerance and sectarianism that the established religions have encountered. There is no 'sacred text' or the equivalent of a bible in Druidism, and there is no universally agreed set of beliefs amongst Druids. Rather than it being founded upon doctrine, it urges followers to learn from their own experience of being in the world. Despite this lack of doctrine, there are a number of ideas and beliefs that most Druids hold in common, and that help to define the nature of Druidism today.

Druids share a belief in the fundamentally spiritual nature of life. Some will favour a particular way of understanding the source of this spiritual nature, and may feel themselves to be animists, pantheists, polytheists, monotheists or duotheists. Others will avoid choosing any one conception of Deity, believing that by its very nature this is unknowable by the mind.

Monotheistic Druids believe there is one Deity: either a Goddess or God, or a Being who is better named Spirit or Great Spirit, to remove misleading associations to gender. Other Druids believe that Deity exists as a pair of forces or beings, which they often characterize as the God and Goddess. They are duotheists, and their belief is shared by many Wiccans.

Polytheistic Druids believe that many gods and goddesses exist, while pantheists, like animists, believe that Deity does not exist as one or more personal gods, but is instead present in all things, and is everything. The term pantheist was coined during the Druid Revival period by John Toland, author of *The History of the Druids*. A recent informal Internet survey suggested that most Druids are pantheistic, with smaller numbers favouring polytheistic, monotheistic or duotheistic beliefs.

I follow a polytheistic form of Druidry, which means I experience many different deities rather than a Lord and Lady. Part of honouring my Gods involves learning as much as possible about how the Iron Age tribes of Britain and Ireland lived – their dress, laws, customs, religion etc. I don't do this because I want to live in some fantasy 'olde worlde'. Rather because I feel there was much wisdom in the ethics and ideals of that time. It's about taking the best of the past and incorporating it with modern life. The Druids in the past served their communities; being a Druid, for me, is a statement of social commitment.

Robin Herne, Ipswich

Whether they have chosen to adopt a particular viewpoint or not, the greatest characteristic of most modern-day Druids is their tolerance of diversity: a Druid gathering can bring together people who have widely varying views about the existence or non-existence of one or more gods, and they will happily participate in ceremonies together, celebrate the seasons, and enjoy each others' company. One of the unwritten tenets of Druidism is that none of us has the monopoly on truth, and that diversity is both healthy and natural.

Nature forms such an important focus of their reverence, that whatever beliefs they hold about Deity, all Druids sense the natural world as divine or sacred. Every part of nature – mountains, rivers, trees, flowers, stones and animals, the weather and the winds, the sun, moon and stars – are all sensed as part of the great web of life, with no one creature or aspect of it having supremacy over any other. Unlike religions that are anthropocentric, believing humanity occupies a central role in the scheme of life, this conception is systemic and holistic, and sees humankind as just one part of the wider family of life.

The Otherworld

Although Druids love Nature, and draw inspiration and spiritual nourishment from it, they also believe that the world we see is not the only one that exists. A cornerstone of Druid belief is in the existence of the Otherworld – a realm or realms which exist beyond the reach of the physical senses, but which are nevertheless real. This Otherworld is seen as the place we travel to when we die. But we can also visit it during our lifetime in dreams, in meditation, under hypnosis, or in 'journeying', when in a shamanic trance.

Different Druids will have different views on the nature of this Otherworld, but it is a universally held belief for three reasons. First, all religions or spiritual traditions hold the view that another reality exists beyond the physical world (whereas materialists hold that only matter exists and is real). Second, Celtic mythology, which inspires so much of Druidism, is replete with descriptions of this Otherworld. Third, the existence of the Otherworld is implicit in 'the greatest belief' of the ancient Druids, as reported by the classical writers, who stated that the Druids believed in a process that has been described as reincarnation or metempsychosis (in which a soul lives in a succession of forms, including both human and animal). In between each life in human or animal form the soul rests in the Otherworld.

Death and Rebirth

While a Christian Druid may believe that the soul is only born once on Earth, most Druids adopt the belief of their ancient forebears that the soul undergoes a process of successive reincarnations in human form, though some may believe that the soul can also reincarnate as an animal.

Many Druids share the view of the Celts reported by Philostratus of Tyana in the second century CE that to be born in this world, we have to die in the Otherworld, and conversely, that when we die here, we are born into the Otherworld. For this reason, Druid funerals try to focus on the idea that the soul is experiencing a time of rebirth.

Although all Druids would agree that physical death does not end our existence, there is no set of universally recognized Druid teachings that offer details of how the process of reincarnation or metempsychosis works, or of what happens to us when we travel to the Otherworld in the after-death state. Individual Druid teachers may offer their own understanding of the process, but generally those who are curious need to study the large body of literature that deals with this subject, which includes the classic works of the Tibetan and Egyptian Books of the Dead, the researches of Spiritualism, the more recent studies of near-death experiences, and of hypnotically induced explorations of the between-lives state.[18]

A clue to the purpose behind the process of successive rebirths can be found if we look at the goals of the Druid. Druids seek above all the cultivation of wisdom, creativity and love. A number of lives on earth, rather than just one, gives us the opportunity to develop these qualities within us.

The goal of wisdom is portrayed in two old tales – one the story of Fionn MacCumhaill (Finn MacCool) from Ireland, the other the story of Taliesin from Wales. In both stories wisdom is sought by an older person – in Ireland in the form of the Salmon of Wisdom, in Wales in the form of three drops of inspiration. In both stories a young helper ends up tasting the wisdom so jealously sought by the adults. These tales, rather than simply teaching the virtues of innocence and helpfulness, contain instructions for achieving wisdom encoded within their symbolism and the sequence of events they describe, and for this reason are often used in the teaching of Druidry.

The goal of creativity is also central to Druidism because the Bards have long been seen as participants in Druidry. Many believe that in the old days they transmitted the wisdom of the Druids in song and story, and that with their prodigious memories they knew the genealogies of the tribes and the tales associated with the local landscape. Celtic cultures display a love of art, music and beauty that often evokes an awareness of the Otherworld, and their old Bardic tales depict a world of sensual beauty in which craftspeople and artists are highly honoured. Today, many people are drawn to Druidry because they sense it is a spirituality that can help them develop their creativity. Rather than stressing the idea that this physical life is temporary, and that we should focus on the after-life, Druidism conveys the idea that we are meant to participate fully in life on Earth, and that we are meant to express and share our creativity as much as we can.

Druidry's third aim is to foster love and to broaden our understanding and experience of it, so that we can love widely and deeply. Its reverence for Nature encourages us to love the land, the Earth, the stars and the wild. It also encourages a love of peace: Druids were traditionally peacemakers, and still are. Often Druid ceremonies begin by offering peace to each cardinal direction, there is a Druid's Peace Prayer, and Druids plant Peace Groves. The Druid path also encourages the love of beauty because it cultivates the Bard, the Artist Within and fosters creativity.

The love of Justice is fostered in modern Druidry by being mentioned in 'The Druid's Prayer'. Many believe that the ancient Druids were judges and law-makers, who were more interested in restorative than punitive justice. Druidry also encourages the love of story and myth, and many people today are drawn to it because they recognize the power of storytelling, and sense its potential to heal and enlighten as well as entertain.

Druidism also recognizes the forming power of the past, and in doing this encourages a love of history and a reverence for the ancestors. The love of trees is fundamental in Druidism, too, and as well as studying tree lore, Druids today plant trees and sacred groves, and support reforestation programmes. Druids love stones, too, and build stone circles, collect stones and work with crystals. They love the truth, and seek this in their quest for wisdom and understanding. They love animals, seeing them as sacred, and they study animal lore. They love the body and sexuality, believing both to be sacred.

Druidism also encourages a love of each other by fostering the magic of relationship and community, and above all a love of life, by encouraging celebration and a full commitment to life – it is not a spirituality which tries to help us escape from a full engagement with the world.

Some Druid groups today present their teachings in three grades or streams: those of the Bard, Ovate and Druid. The three goals of love, wisdom and creative expression can be related to the work of these three streams. Bardic teachings help to develop our creativity, Ovate teachings help to develop our love for the natural world and the community of all life, and Druid teachings help us in our quest for wisdom.

Living in the World

The real test of the value of a spiritual path lies in the degree to which it can help us live our lives in the world. It needs to be able to provide us with inspiration, counsel and encouragement as we negotiate the sometimes difficult and even tragic events that can occur during a lifetime.

The primary philosophical posture of Druidism is one of respect towards life. A word often used by Druids to describe this approach is reverence, which expands the concept of respect to include an awareness of the sacred. By being reverent towards human beings, for example, Druids treat the body, relationships and sexuality with respect and as sacred. Reverence should not be confused with piousness or a lack of vigorous engagement – true reverence is strong and sensual as well as gentle and kind.

This attitude of reverence and respect extends to all creatures. Many Druids will either be vegetarian, or will eat meat, but oppose factory-farming methods. For many Druids today the primary position of love and respect towards all creatures extends to include a desire to avoid harming others. In Wicca, a Pagan path which, though different, has much in common with Druidry, this idea is expressed in the Wiccan Rede as 'Do what you like, so long as you harm no one'.[19] The idea that we should avoid harming others is enshrined in Eastern traditions in the doctrine of *Ahimsa*, or Non-Violence, and was first described in around 800 BCE in the Hindu scriptures, the Upanishads. Jains, Hindus and Buddhists all teach this doctrine, which became popular in the West following the non-violent protests of Mahatma Gandhi.

The Parehaka Maori protest movement in New Zealand and the campaigns of Martin Luther King in the USA also helped to spread the idea of *Ahimsa* around the world. In Britain, one particular Druid group has specialized in non-violent protest – the Loyal Arthurian Warband led by Arthur Pendragon, who believes he is a reincarnation of King Arthur. The Warband has protested for free access to Stonehenge at the Druid festival times, and against road-building projects which threaten sacred sites. Arthur Pendragon was the first British citizen to chal-

lenge the 1994 Criminal Justice Act, which gave chief consta-
bles the power to disperse gatherings even if peaceful. In a
triumph for justice, the judge dismissed the charge against
Arthur.

Many Druids today adopt a stance which abstains from
harming others, and which focuses on the idea of Peace. They
draw their inspiration from the classical accounts of the Druids,
which portrayed them as mediators who abstained from war,
and who urged peace on opposing armies. Julius Caesar wrote:
'For they generally settle all their disputes, both public and private . . . The Druids usually abstain from war, nor do they pay
taxes together with the others; they have exemption from war-
fare.' And Diodorus Siculus wrote: 'Often when the combatants
are ranged face to face, and swords are drawn and spears are
bristling, these men come between the armies and stay the
battle, just as wild beasts are sometimes held spellbound. Thus
even among the most savage barbarians anger yields to wisdom,
and Mars is shamed before the Muses.'

In addition Druids today can follow the example of one of
the most important figures in the modern Druid movement,
Ross Nichols, who in common with many of the world's greatest
thinkers and spiritual teachers, upheld the doctrines of non-
violence and pacifism. Many of Nichols' contemporaries, who
shared similar interests in Celtic mythology, were also pacifists,
including the composer Michael Tippett and T. H. White, the
author of the Arthurian *The Once & Future King*. Nichols often
used to finish essays he wrote with the simple sign-off: 'Peace to
all beings.'

The two attitudes of Peace and Love, which many Druids
hold as fundamental to their conduct in life, are the same two
ideals that were championed by the alternative culture of the
1960s – whose proponents are now the middle-aged generation

of 'baby boomers'. This is no coincidence. The ideals of the six-ties were informed by Romanticism, and Romanticism drew upon the two sources of inspiration of the Druids: the world of Nature and the world of Story. Via Romanticism, a thread of ideas connects this oldest of traditions, Druidism, to the ideals and values of twentieth-century counter-culture. Many baby boomers know in their hearts that their ideals were worthy, but feel dejected or cynical about how they have been abandoned in favour of consumerism and the demands of living in the modern world. It is easy to interpret Peace and Love as 'soft' or passive qualities, but Druidism offers a way of reconnecting to these values that renders them potent and proactive, and trans-lates them into specific actions in our everyday lives.

The Web of Life and the Illusion of Separateness

Woven into much of Druid thinking and all of its practice is the belief that we are all connected in a universe that is essentially benign – that we do not exist as isolated beings who must fight to survive in a cruel world. Instead we are seen as part of a great web or fabric of life that includes every living creature and all of Creation. This is essentially a pantheistic view of life, which sees all of Nature as sacred and as interconnected.

This view has become popular recently thanks to the work of James Lovelock whose Gaia hypothesis suggests that the planet is a living being, functioning as a single organism which main-tains the conditions necessary for its survival. The various processes that occur on Earth – physical, chemical, geological, and biological – are seen as interconnected, each affecting the other in a continuous process of exchange and relationship.

During the 1980s, the Gaia hypothesis, together with theo-ries proposed by quantum physicists like Fritjof Capra, began to add scientific perspectives to a theory that many believed were articulated a century earlier by the Native American leader, Chief Seattle. The moving words attributed to him inspired people all over the world, and awoke them to the idea of inter-connectedness:

> This we know: The Earth does not belong to man; man belongs to the Earth. This we know. All things are connected like the blood which unites one family. All things are connected. Whatever befalls the earth befalls the sons of the earth. Man did not weave the web of life: he is merely a strand in it. Whatever he does to the web, he does to himself.

It is now known that these words were written by the screen-writer Ted Perry for a 1972 film about ecology. They cannot be found in the first recorded version of the speech made in 1887. But the ideas conveyed by Perry's version strike a chord in almost everyone – perhaps because of an innate sense that they are indeed true, perhaps because this view is the one that has been held by our forebears for millennia.

Certainly we find this understanding in Anglo-Saxon times, when the 'Web of Wyrd' was pictured as a great web of invisi-ble fibres that connect everything, and along which the wizard or shaman may travel. A similar idea lies at the basis of the Western Mystery Tradition, in which each individual is seen as a microcosm, or tiny replica, of the Universe – the macrocosm. Changes that we effect within ourselves are then believed to affect the macrocosm – the greater whole, with both the micro- and macrocosm being inextricably linked.

Now that science is starting to explore our interconnected-ness, traditional barriers between disciplines are starting to break down. We increasingly understand the limitations of studying subjects in isolation. Just as the individual grows from the stage of dependence through independence to an awareness of their interdependence, so the same may be happening collectively. From being dependent upon dogma and direction from the authority figures of church and state, we learned from the age of the Enlightenment onwards to manifest our individuality, until now we are starting to discover that in reality we live in an interdependent world, where no one can truly be an island.

Druids often experience this belief in their bodies and hearts rather than simply in their minds. They find themselves feeling increasingly at home in the world – and when they walk out onto the land and look up at the moon or stars, or smell the coming rain on the wind they feel in the fabric of their beings that they are a part of the family of life, that they are 'home', and that they are not alone.

Here is how one practitioner expresses this:

As a Druid I learn the language of stones and trees. I hear the whistle of the Red Tail Hawk who brings a fierce clarity in moments of confusion. No longer a separate consciousness, as I walk through woods and meadows, I am a part of the fabric, woven into the pattern. There is no hierarchy of human before animal or plant before stone.

I listen to the trees and the voices of the wind in the trees. I stand still in the path as my dog snuffs ahead of me, and I feel the breath, and the speech of the wind as spirit voices. I watch the beech leaves which cling to the branches in winter, shake their hands, hundreds of tiny parchment palms on silver arms. They tremble in a chorus of declaration: 'This is always here, do not underestimate the power of the spirit which wanders these tracks.' I am rewoven in the woods . . .

The consequences of feeling integrated into the fabric of life are profound. Apart from this trusting posture towards life bringing benefits in psychological and physical health for the individual, there are benefits to society too. Abuse and exploitation comes from the illusion of separateness. Once you believe that you are part of the family of life, and that all things are connected, the values of love and reverence for life naturally follow, as does the practice of peacefulness and harmlessness.

The Law of the Harvest

Related to the idea that we are all connected in one great web of life is the belief held by most Druids that whatever we do in the world creates an effect which will ultimately also affect us. Wiccan beliefs are often similar to Druid ones. Just as the doctrine of harmlessness is expressed in the maxim 'Do what you like, so long as you harm no one', so the idea that our actions may rebound on us is presented as the 'Law of the Threefold Return', which suggests that the effect of our actions or intentions will return to us threefold. A similar idea (avoiding the mathematical precision of the Wiccan maxim which runs the risk of being interpreted literally) is found in many different traditions and cultures: folk wisdom in Britain and America says that 'what goes around comes around' and in ancient Egypt, the idea attributed to Jesus when he said 'As ye sow, so shall ye reap' was spoken by the god Thoth several thousand years earlier in the *Egyptian Book of the Dead*, when he said 'Truth is the harvest scythe. What is sown – love or anger or bitterness – that shall be your bread. The corn is no better than its seed, then let what you plant be good.' In Hinduism and Buddhism the idea is expressed as the doctrine of cause and effect, or karma.

The two beliefs – that all is connected and that we will harvest the consequences of our actions – come naturally to
Druids, because they represent ideas that evolve out of an observation of the natural world. Just as the feeling of our being part
of the great web of life can come to us as we gaze in awe at the
beauty of nature, so the awareness that we will reap the consequences of our actions also comes to us as we observe the
processes of sowing and harvesting.

In summary, most Druids today will hold to the following six
core beliefs: the importance of tolerance and accepting diversity
of opinion and belief; the existence of Spirit or Deity; the existence of the Otherworld; the process of Rebirth; the Web of
Life; and the Law of the Harvest.

6

Mysticism, Shamanism and Magic

Becoming Druid, taking to the Druid Way, does not depend on some hidden and closely guarded lore any more than it depends on surface manifestations. A Druid is inspired by the most essential, bright, open and accessible of sources.

Greywind, *The Voice within the Wind – of Becoming and the Druid Way*

Some people follow Druidism as a spiritual or philosophical approach to life: they like the way that it respects Nature, the way it offers no dogma, has no creed, and is open to members of all faiths and none. They don't feel the necessity to 'have' a religion, or they share John Lennon's vision when he sang, in 'Imagine', of an ideal world with no religion. Others practise one of the mainstream religions but also feel themselves to be Druids – and so there are Christian or Buddhist Druids, for example. Still others follow Druidism as a religion in its own right. American Druid groups in particular often relate to Druidry as a neo-Pagan religion. Isaac Bonewits, a key figure in US Druidry, writes:

'In ADF we believe that excellence in clergy training and practice is vital for any healthy, growing religion. [In the future] we see talented and well-trained Neopagan clergy leading thousands of people in effective magical and mundane actions to save endangered species, stop polluters, and preserve wilderness. We see our healers saving thousands of lives and our Bards inspiring millions through music and video concerts and dramas. We see Neopaganism as a mass religion, changing social, political, and environmental attitudes around the world.'

I'm one of those who sees Druidry as a spiritual/philosophical approach. I have never been comfortable with organized religions; indeed, given the long history of horrendous deeds done in the name of various religions, I have often wondered if the positive aspects could possibly outweigh the negatives.

Still, I have always felt deeply spiritual, and I do believe in Deity. And since I tend toward pantheism in my perception, Druidry has been ideal for me. I also appreciate the inclusiveness of Druidry, because I am not arrogant enough to believe that my opinions on religions must be shared by all.

K. H., Louisiana, USA

Despite the ambitious enthusiasm of Bonewits' ideas, the majority of Americans join groups based in Britain which see Druidry less as a specific religion, and more as a spiritual path that can be followed in a variety of ways, depending upon the needs of the seeker. In this approach, the Druid Way is often understood as a path of initiation that can help the individual achieve their mystical, shamanic or magical goals.

The belief that there is more to life than the world of appearances, that an Otherworld exists, leads logically to the belief that we can make contact with forces and beings that exist beyond the world of appearances. Many people have had experiences of 'extrasensory perception' – even if only fleetingly, perhaps just once or twice in their lives. And a significant proportion of people have had experiences of making contact, or of being aware of the presence of loved ones after they have died.

Some people feel that an exploration of the Otherworld or of 'other dimensions' is not for them, and it may even scare them to contemplate making such an attempt. But for others, nothing could be more exciting. Like explorers, they may sense there is some risk (of delusion, madness or the disappointment of failure) but their inherent curiosity drives them forward.

This desire to explore the world beyond the 'veil of appearances' has always existed – holy people, shamans and wizards in every culture have discovered a host of ways to open the 'doors of perception,' as Aldous Huxley put it, and to travel through those doors. They have meditated, eaten magic mushrooms, smoked herbs, created hallucinogenic brews from roots, plants and animals, danced or drummed until they entered a trance, fasted or retreated into solitude for months or years on end – all in the hopes of breaking through or out of the matrix of 'consensus reality' to achieve an experience of realities or states of consciousness beyond the everyday.

Mystic and Shaman

For some their sole spiritual desire is to unite with Deity, however they conceive of this: as God, Goddess, Great Spirit or Ultimate Cause. To such a mystic there is as little point exploring the complexities and different levels of the

Otherworld as there is to exploring the world of appearances. They are interesting, perhaps, but ultimately a distraction, because from the mystic's viewpoint the only truly real thing is Deity.

Others believe that every level of reality offers valid and valuable experiences, and want to travel beyond the veil of appearances, not to shun the seductions of the Otherworld and travel straight to the heart of Deity, but instead to explore the treasures and to experience the learning they hope to find in that Otherworld. This is the shamanic as opposed to the mystical approach to spiritual development and exploration. Although the term 'shamanism' comes originally from the term used to describe the practice of traditional Siberian healer-magicians, in recent times its use has broadened into what Michael Harner, a world authority on shamanism, has called 'a method to open a door and enter a different reality'. Some contemporary writers even talk about 'Celtic shamanism' when they refer to certain practices mentioned in Celtic literature that help the seeker enter different realities and return with visions, insights or information.

One of the appealing qualities of Druidry is its versatility. It offers a context for a wide variety of approaches to spiritual development. Even though mystics shun the seductions of both this world and the Otherworld, they will usually use prayers, imagery and exercises from a particular tradition to help them in their quest. So Druid mystics will use Celtic or Druid rituals, images and prayers. Those who are more shamanically inclined will add to these elements the use of guided meditations, trance work, dancing or drumming to achieve their aim of entering other states of awareness – a process which is often termed 'journeying' and which has also been called 'astral travelling'.

Shamanic Journeying

During these journeys, encounters often occur with Otherworldly beings, such as an ancestor, a deceased relative or friend, or a spirit guide, who may appear as an animal, a human or in some other form. Sceptics may consider these experiences the result of an excessively vivid imagination, but those who have taken these journeys often experience profound insights and healing. Sometimes these shamanic experiences occur spontaneously – when in a dream we meet a being who gives us healing or advice, or when awake we become aware of someone who has died counselling or consoling us. But those who follow Druidry as a shamanic path attempt deliberately to make contact with the Otherworld – to take the belief that 'all is connected' literally, and begin to explore certain of these links and connections.

Some teachers work with drums, encouraging those present to travel on the beat of the drum to the Otherworld, while others will use the power of their voice to guide the listeners' awareness. Either of these techniques will usually be embedded within a ritual designed to establish a sense of being within a sacred space, and to evoke the guidance and protection of Deity or deities, and perhaps Otherworldly guardians or spirits. Dance, sacred movements or gestures, and chanting may be used during the ceremony, and ritual objects, candles, incense, statues and pictures might be employed to enhance the participants' awareness of the sacred. The ritual might also take place within a Celtic sweat house, which – like a Native American sweat lodge – creates a powerful environment for undertaking such work. Until the nineteenth century, the Irish used sweathouses fuelled by peat, which they called Tigh 'n' Alluis. Today a wood-burning stove or heated stones are used.

The Path of Magic

There is yet one more way in which Druidry can be pursued – as a path of magic. The magical approach in Druidry, like the mystical and shamanic, follows from the belief that 'all is connected' and that other worlds or dimensions exist in addition to the realm of appearances. But it also takes into consideration the view that we are meant to be here, that we are destined to be active, creative participants in life, and that our thoughts, feelings, words and actions all have an effect which obeys the Law of the Harvest. Like ripples in a pool caused by a stone falling into it, the magician sees each person as an influential being, who can cause either joy or sorrow by the way that they live their lives.

Many people think of magic either as the creation of illusion, as in stage magic, or as the attempt to manipulate circumstances or people through spell-casting in order to obtain things, such as love or wealth. But there is another type of magic that is much more interesting and which involves at its heart sensing life as awe-inspiring, as magical in the best sense of the word. From this perspective Druidism offers ideas and techniques that can enhance one's awareness of life as magical, and can make the practice of magic a conscious attempt to assume responsibility for our thoughts, words and deeds. The world then becomes a magical place, and one's life a magical journey that takes place within it.

Two concepts in Druidry are helpful in pursuing the magical path. In the Asterix cartoon books the Druid Getafix is often seen stirring a cauldron to create a magical elixir that will confer superhuman strength on Asterix, the hero of the tale. Such an elixir does exist in Druidry – not in the form of an actual liquid, but in the form of an energy which is seen as bringing illumination, inspiration and wisdom. Known as *Awen* in Welsh, and *Imbas* in Irish, Druids sense this as a universal force which flows through the world and which can be encouraged to flow through us to bring us these gifts. The words 'Imbas' and 'Awen' are chanted in ceremonies or meditation, and the study of this force, and how to encourage it in our lives, forms the basis of much Druid training.

Another force is said to exist too – *Nwyfre*, which is a Welsh word, deriving from an ancient Celtic word *Naomh*, meaning 'firmament' or 'heavens'. Nwyfre is the life force that flows through the Universe, and which is called Chi or Qi in China and Prana in India.

By cultivating the flow of Nwyfre and Awen, the Druid aims to improve their physical vitality and their creative ability. In doing this, the Druid has access to two powerful 'elixirs' which can aid him or her in a work which is essentially alchemical. Alchemy, as a branch of magic, can be practised either as an external or as an internal art. Used externally it attempts to manipulate matter to create gold. Used internally it attempts to transform the alchemist, symbolically or metaphorically, into gold. Rather than working with the energies of Awen and Nwyfre to manipulate events or circumstances, the Druid uses these forces to transform themselves. Ironically, this often has the effect of changing outer circumstances more effectively than any attempt to manipulate them directly, because our circumstances often depend upon our internal states, and until our internal state changes, attempts to alter external conditions will often be simply palliative and short-lived.

Some people avoid anything which is labelled magical. Yet, once we understand the way in which magic is used and understood in Druidry, we can see that it involves an ethical attempt to take responsibility for the fact that we are causal beings – that we affect the world around us, whether we are conscious of this or not.

There are two ways that we can work magically with Druidry. The first could be termed passive and involves adopting an attitude of awe and reverence towards life and the world. This 'way of being' is also a way of seeing, as the writer Marcel Proust expressed so well when he said: 'The real magic lies not in seeking new landscapes but in having new eyes.' When we see and understand life to be magical, we start to experience it as magical in our hearts and souls too.

The second way could be termed active and involves becoming aware of the creative power that we possess simply by being alive, and then consciously working to use that creative power in the service of our values and ideals. Here we can see how the goals of the Druid to work towards love, wisdom and creativity can become in themselves magical goals.

7

Ethics and Values

For the most part, Druid ethics are not much different from Christian or Buddhist ethics. What sets modern Druid ethics apart is that it de-emphasizes blind trust and obedience to authorities, rejects the idea that there are any scriptures that are more sacred than others, and grounds its ideal of respect and love in the whole natural world, not just the human community.

Alferian Gwydion MacLir, from a Message Board
discussion on Druid Ethics on www.druidry.org

The classical author Strabo wrote that the Druids studied 'moral philosophy'.[20] The author Brendan Myers concludes that the first moral principle of the ancient Druids was a devotion to truth. In the Testament of Morann, a document traced to the period between the seventh and ninth centuries CE, but which seems to emerge out of the pre-Christian Druidic period, advice is given on how a prince should rule:

Let him magnify Truth, it will magnify him.
Let him strengthen Truth, it will strengthen him.

. . . Through the ruler's Truth massive mortalities are averted
from men.

. . . Through the ruler's Truth all the land is fruitful and
childbirth worthy.

Through the ruler's Truth there is abundance of tall corn.

St Patrick was said to have asked Oisin, the son of Fionn
MacCumhaill, what sustained his people before the advent of
Christianity, to which he replied: 'The truth that was in our
hearts, and strength in our arms, and fulfilment in our tongues.'
Myers concludes: 'It is interesting that he should cite truth first,
as though truth had an overriding place in the culture. This evidence leads me to believe that the first moral principle of
Druidism is this: in a situation where a moral decision must be
made, we should always choose truth, in the expansion and
enrichment of human knowledge, in ourselves and others, and
at all levels of our being.'[21]

In the final analysis, though, Myers suggests that the Druids
may not have adhered to specific rules and authorities to deter-
mine proper ethical conduct. Instead he sees them striving to
become a certain kind of person, out of whom ethical behaviour
naturally arises.

Athelia Nihtscada also turns to Irish source material to
explore Druid ethics. The old Brehon laws, which were
recorded by Christian clerics in the fifth century CE, pre-
dated Christianity and offer a fascinating insight into early
Irish society. By studying these laws and seeing how they
might be applicable to modern living, Nihtscada has articulated eleven principles or codes of conduct for the
contemporary Druid:

1 Every action has a consequence that must be observed and you must be prepared to compensate for your actions if required.

2 All life is sacred and all are responsible for seeing that this standard is upheld.

3 You do still live in society and are bound by its rules.

4 Work with high standards.

5 Make an honest living.

6 Be a good host as well as a good guest.

7 Take care of yourself. (Health was held in high esteem amongst the Celts, so much that a person could be fined for being grossly overweight due to lack of care.)

8 Serve your community.

9 Maintain a healthy balance between the spiritual and worldly. (Nihtscad writes: 'Ethical and self-respecting Druids did nothing without being properly schooled or aware of the consequences ahead of time. They knew when it was appropriate to visit the Otherworld and immerse themselves in the spiritual as well as when it was appropriate to be fully in this world.')

10 Uphold the Truth, starting with yourself.

11 Be sure in your convictions, particularly when judging or accusing someone, but also when debating. Ask yourself: are you really sure? Do you really know that this is the case?[22]

Apart from the work of Myers and Nihtscad, little has been written about ethics in contemporary Druidism since most Druids are keen to avoid the problems caused by dictating a morality to others. So much suffering has resulted throughout history because one group of people have decided that it is good to do one thing and bad to do another. Just as most

Druids have avoided dictating which type of theology someone should adopt, so too have they avoided telling each other, or the world, how to behave.

Over the years, though, I have noticed that most Druids have a highly developed sense of ethical behaviour, which is usually implicit in their actions, rather than explicitly stated. A person can only act ethically if they hold to certain values, and by talking about these values we can avoid the pitfall of suggesting ethical guidelines which can then so easily turn into a dogma. Instead of imposing a code of conduct upon people, we can return to Myers' suggestion to practise a Druidry that helps us become a certain kind of person, out of whom ethical behaviour naturally arises.

Druidry asks us, above all, to open ourselves to the inspiration and beauty of Nature and Art, through its celebration of creativity. By nourishing ourselves through contact with the natural world and with art of every kind, and by holding to the core beliefs of Druidism already outlined, a number of qualities emerge as values that can form the basis of ethical decisions and behaviour. In particular, the following four qualities represent core values that are fostered by following Druidism as a spiritual path today: responsibility, community, trust and integrity.

It is easy to see ourselves as victims in life – as tiny cogs in a vast and impersonal machine driven by others for economic and political ends. But by holding to the belief that everything is connected, that another reality exists beyond the everyday physical world, and that everything we think, feel or do has an effect, the Druid is able to assume an attitude of responsibility, and to feel empowered to be of value in the world. Like everyone else, they will sometimes feel the victim of others or of circumstances. While that feeling may come and go, the predominant belief will be that each of us is a causal being who exists in a web of life that unites every living creature. This means that each of us can choose to act as a force for good in the world.

The Druid will tend to see many of the world's problems emerging from a refusal to take responsibility and to act for the greater good of the whole. By not taking responsibility for environmental degradation, for example, they see politicians and corporations acting simply for the short-term gains of power and profit. Many political systems and most corporations do not encourage the taking of individual responsibility or the value of personal empowerment. Instead they need consumption and compliance. Druidism encourages the taking of individual responsibility – first in our own lives, then in concert with others for our community, and for the wider issues that affect the community of all life.

Taking responsibility for our thoughts, feelings and actions fosters an attitude of responsibility towards others, and the world needs responsible people now more than ever.

Increasing urbanization, population growth, the commercialization of culture, the development of consumerism and globalization, have all tended to undermine our sense of living in a community, close to our fellow human beings, close to animals and the land. Many people are drawn to Druidry because they find it helps them get back in touch with 'the circle of all Beings'. By its reverential attitude to Nature, by its belief in the sacredness of all creatures, and by its belief in the holistic relationship between all things, Druidry fosters the value of community, of relationship with others.

There will be times when we need solitude and, like all spiritual paths, Druidry recognizes the need for retreats, when we let go of our concerns for others and focus instead on our personal quest or upon Deity. But Druidry is not a path that advocates a permanent detachment from others or the world. Instead it urges a pro-active and enthusiastic, Awen-filled engagement with others and the world, seeing life on earth as meaningful and purposeful – as an adventure to be undertaken rather than as a prison from which we should escape, or as a bridge we should simply cross.

There will be times when a Druid feels alone, isolated or alienated from others. While that feeling may come and go, holding to the value of community will enable them to return to a bedrock of feeling and belief in which they are part of one family – the web of life, the circle of all Beings.

> I would love to live
> Like a river flows,
> Carried by the surprise
> Of its own unfolding.
>   John O'Donohue

Coming to place a value in community and in being in relationship with the circle of all Beings comes from the simple observation of Nature, and the way in which everything is connected. In a similar way, contemplating the flow of a river brings us to the value of trust. It is a common experience among people who are aware of the spiritual dimension to find that when they trust in life they find it easier to enter a 'flow' which carries their life along with a quality of lightness, joy and effortlessness, that also keeps them aligned with their spiritual purpose. Of course trust will sometimes give way to its opposite – mistrust and fear – but by believing that life is fundamentally good, that there is meaning and purpose to existence, the spiritual seeker finds it increasingly easy to come back to the position of trust.

The more we can trust in life, the more we can encourage this flow. Experiencing the inspiration of Awen as a flow is common for creative people – when they are inspired they feel creative energy literally flowing through their bodies and they commonly report that all they need to do is trust and get their thinking minds out of the way, so that the flow can continue and creation can occur. Likewise with Nwyfre – when we are full of health and vitality, we feel as if the life force is flowing freely and clearly through us. When we are unwell that force no longer flows, and we can sometimes sense blockages of energy in our body.

By affirming the value of trust, and by returning constantly to this position, whatever setbacks may occur, our life – the decisions we make, the relationships we form – begins to be built on trust rather than on fear: on the need to conform, to maintain status, or to protect ourselves, for example.

The magical understanding of Druidry, that our state of being influences the world around us, tells us that as we connect to the value of trust in life, this trust will start to radiate, and will in its turn attract trust from others, generating a beneficent cycle.

Although the term integrity is often used to mean 'the quality of possessing and steadfastly adhering to high moral principles and professional standards', its deeper meaning is defined in the dictionary as 'the state of being complete and undivided. The state of being sound or undamaged.' Before a mission is sent into space, for example, the integrity of the spacecraft is checked again and again.

Used in this deeper sense, integrity becomes a value or quality sought by Druids, just as it is by all spiritual seekers. The spiritual journey begins for us when we sense that we are lacking something. We feel incomplete, and so we begin to strive towards Deity, enlightenment, wholeness. Further along the track we discover that these realities exist within us and that it is only our mind that believes we are separated from them. Slowly, through meditation and spiritual practice, we open to an awareness of our completeness, our wholeness. We find integrity. And from this place of integrity we can act with authenticity – not trying to be someone other than who we simply are.

Again, as with all these qualities, there will be times when we lose our sense of integrity, when we feel desperately incomplete or divided, and when we act not honestly and from our deepest feelings but inauthentically out of fear or misunderstanding. But one of the values of following a spiritual path lies in its acting as a gentle reminder, and offering particular disciplines that bring us back to a contemplation of these core qualities. In this way, over time, our experience of a lack of any quality will start to diminish as our spiritual life connects us to these core values.

It is important to understand, however, that the holistic stance of Druidry does not deny the value or purpose of experiencing difficulty or discomfort. Our depth of humanity comes precisely from our experiencing the contrasts of life: without the experience of unhappiness we would not be able to fully appreciate happiness. Maturity of character and soul seems to require some amount of suffering, and we need to experience – ideally in small and manageable doses – the lack of each of the qualities discussed, so that we can experience the feeling and effects of irresponsibility, alienation, disempowerment, fear and lack of integrity, in order to be complete human beings.

In the end values or principles such as those stated here, with others that are related to or flow from them – such as honour, courage and respect – can form the basis out of which ethical and moral decisions can be made. Rather than internalizing a moral code developed perhaps centuries ago by the ruling religious or political elite, we can develop a strong individual sense of morality and ethics born out of our own inner connection to such values. Blaise Pascal succinctly summarized, in the following triad, the ingredients we need to develop this morality, when he said simply: 'Heart, instinct, principles.'

8

What Do Druids Do?

Environmentalism, when conceived as a spiritual path and grounded in an ancestral tradition such as Druidry, can be a powerful force for healing in this world.

Brendan Myers, *Dangerous Religion – Environmental Spirituality and Its Activist Dimension*

The Seasonal Festivals

At the heart of Druidism lies a love of Nature and of her changing face as the seasons turn. Eight times a year, once every six weeks or so, Druids participate in a celebration that expresses this devotion to the natural world. These seasonal festivals can be large public events with hundreds of adults and children gathering at sacred sites, such as Stonehenge, Avebury or Glastonbury, or they can be very private events celebrated by a single Druid in their garden or living room, or by a small group of Druids and friends who have gathered together in a park or garden.

These eight seasonal festivals consist of the solstices and equinoxes: four moments during the year which are dictated by the relationship between the Earth and Sun, and the four cross-quarter day festivals which are not determined astronomically, but are related to the traditional pastoral calendar.

The summer and winter solstices are celebrated when the sun is nearest and furthest from the Earth. The summer solstice is on the longest day of the year, 21 or 22 June. The winter solstice is on the shortest day of year, 21 or 22 December. The equinoxes occur when day and night are equal: on 21 or 22 March in spring and 21 or 22 September in autumn. In the southern hemisphere these dates are reversed.

The other four festivals are also related to the seasons, but are not tied to specific astronomical events. Instead they have evolved from traditional festival times linked to farming practices begun in western Europe thousands of years ago: lambing in early February, bringing the cattle out to pasture in early May, the start of the harvest at the beginning of August, and the preparations for winter at the end of October.

Druids observe this eightfold cycle of festivals by meeting together, or celebrating on their own. Sometimes the celebration will be informal – a picnic with friends, or a party during which someone will speak about the time of year and its significance, accompanied perhaps by storytelling, music or poetry. At other times the celebration will be formal. When the Order of Bards, Ovates and Druids celebrates the summer solstice at Stonehenge, for example, a hundred or so participants will walk, robed and in silence, three times around the great trilithons before entering the inner circle of stones to stand together in a circle. After three notes from a replica Bronze-Age horn, known as a dord, each of the cardinal directions will be greeted, and then the meaning of the solstice will be explained, followed by a meditation and Eisteddfod of music and poetry.

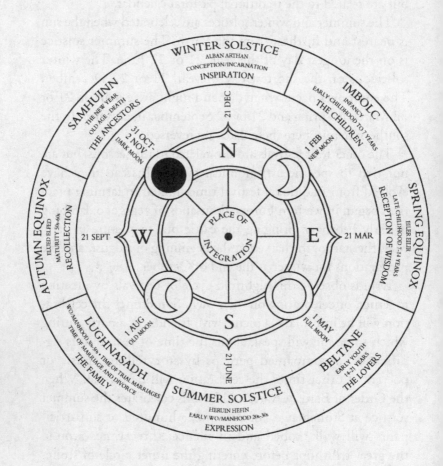

The Eight Festivals and the Wheel of the Year

At other times, though, the celebrations combine a formal ritual with informal elements, such as on Glastonbury Tor when several hundred adults and children gather together in a circle for a solstice celebration. Some people will be wearing robes of different colours and design, others will be dressed in everyday clothes. A circle will be cast by children scattering petals or blowing bubbles. A fire eater will bless the circle with fire, and someone will sprinkle everyone with water from Chalice Well as a further blessing. The ritual itself is formal, in the sense that it has been prepared in advance and includes traditional elements, but the ambience is informal and joyful. Every so often all participants will spontaneously cheer, laugh or clap, and at the closing of the ceremony the crowd will gather in clusters to sit and chat, to admire the view, or to picnic together.

Often Druid festivals include a central section known by the Welsh word 'Eisteddfod', which offers a time for the expression of creativity by anyone in the circle. Although certain participants may guide the festival, and have various roles within it (such as casting or blessing the circle) no one is acting as a priest or priestess, in the sense of being an intermediary between the other participants and Deity.

Some forms of Druidism, particularly in the USA, have a different approach and model themselves on the revealed religions' use of concepts such as clergy and laity, but the contemporary Druidry that has emerged out of Britain over the last forty years favours a different and more egalitarian approach, in the belief that attempts to create a 'priest/esshood' are fraught with difficulties, with the risks of ego inflation, mystification and the disempowerment of those not within the 'inner circle' of the 'elect'.

The purpose of celebrating the eight seasonal festivals is to create a pattern or rhythm in our year that allows for a few hours' pause every six weeks or so in our busy and often stressful routine, so that we can open to the magic of being alive on this earth at this special time. It gives us a chance to fully enter the moment, to connect with the life of the land around us, and to feel the influence of the season in our bodies, hearts and minds. If we celebrate on our own, it is a time when we can enter into meditation, perhaps reviewing our life since the last festival, thinking forward to the next one, then returning to open ourselves fully to the Here and Now.

In addition to observing the eightfold cycle, each Druid will develop a personal practice that is suited to their needs and their circumstances. This will also change over time. One person may live on their own and have a good deal of free time, while another might have a young family and work long hours. One person may relate to Druidry as a philosophy and devote much of their time to reading and study, while others will want a more hands-on experience – and will spend their time communing with Nature in the woods and on the land. Some people like ritual, others find it distracting. Some like praying, reading or meditating, others don't.

Here the novelist Barbara Erskine describes how her discovery of Druidry led to a regular practice that combines Druidism with her Christian faith:

Druidry acted as a change of focus for me; a personal reinterpretation; an altered attitude. It shone a beam of light into a monochrome landscape and reminded me of an ancient church where Celtic saints had called blessings onto rain-soaked hills, where St Kevin allowed a blackbird to nest on his hand, where Brighid was both goddess and saint, a church where Our Lady was also the Star of the Sea, a blessed feminine warmth which a more puritan faith had distanced. Ancient prayers took on deeper meanings for me. Now the Benedicite *read like a Celtic hymn.*

The Druidical circle of seasons was there within the liturgy, sacred geometry was there, though forgotten by most, as were the healing energies of stone and stained glass and the mysticism of ancient words.

Historians and theologians may find the belief untenable but I like the idea of long-ago Druids segueing neatly with the changing focus of the heavens into a Celtic Christianity. It feels right.

My practice of meditation evolved naturally back into one of regular prayer and though prayer can happen every- and any where I set up a small altar of my own again. In its centre I have a beautiful statue made by a friend, of the Blessed Virgin, not a meek, mild obedient role model, but Queen of Heaven, with crown and royal robes. On her knee is the Christ child. At the four corners of the altar I have put symbols of earth, air, fire and water. There is a Celtic cross there, and flowers. Sometimes I have incense, sometimes meditation oils. Sometimes this is the centre of my Druid rituals. I use it as a place to pray, to meditate and to listen. Unorthodox? Probably. But it makes perfect sense to me.

Druidry offers a wealth of techniques – not one single practice that must be performed regularly. Out of this wealth each Druid can develop a practice that best suits them. Some people who lead busy lives may find that years go by when they simply gather with friends at each of the eight festival times, and at other times occasionally meditate or use a Druid divination system, such as the *Ogham Tree Oracle* or the *Druid Animal Oracle*, when trying to gain insight into particular problems. (While some Druids create their own oracles, these can also be purchased in published form – see Further Reading Section on page 108). In contrast, there will be those who feel the need for a daily practice. They will often create an altar in their homes or a sacred space in their gardens in which they can perform a simple ritual to open their awareness to the sacred, to connect with the energies of Earth, Trees, Sea and Sky. Some will then meditate within the atmosphere created by the ritual, others might pray, or read devotional material, inspiring poetry or Celtic blessings for example, or select a card from a Druid divination system and meditate on the guidance offered by it. A wide range of ceremonies, meditations and techniques are available.

The most valuable and life-changing practice of all, though, evolves gradually and simply as a different way of being in the world. Through working with Druid teachings and ceremonies, changes occur in our attitudes, feelings and behaviour which enable us to live more and more frequently in alignment with our sense of purpose and meaning, and with an awareness of the inherent spirituality of all life. This may sound simple, but the consequences of achieving, or of working towards this state are profound. We enter a beneficent cycle, in which the more we express the core values of Druidry, the more we find these reflected back to us in the events and relationships in our life. As this way of being evolves it becomes possible to find those elusive qualities of serenity and happiness, and to be of service to others and the world around us.

Here is what one practitioner has to say about her practice of Druidry:

> Eight times a year I stand in circle with my grove of friends and fellow Druids as we celebrate the wheel of the year. As the seasons turn, so our circle turns. Our hands reach out and touch as the light grows in strength and as darkness takes a turn, to grow and recede. At the darkest point, the light returns, and at the brightest moment, darkness begins to grow. In darkness I look up to see the belt of Orion and his blue dog Sirius, or the Seven Sisters, and know I too am part of their ancient story.
>
> When I celebrate the seasons, I find fellowship in the mineral, plant, animal and human community. For me the practice of Druidry is a way of looking at life which allows a place for all. Step by step this has allowed me to integrate many facets in my life story, to widen the circle of my self acceptance. I have developed a livelihood which has evolved from my Druid studies. I have a framework for political and social actions. My hope for the future lies in the resilience I have experienced in the natural world.

Pilgrimage and Sacred Sites

In addition to any practice a Druid might incorporate into their everyday lives, there may also be times when it seems important to make a special journey. The call to go on a pilgrimage has been felt by people of all spiritual traditions throughout history. In times of crisis or stagnation, or to mark special events, or simply in response to an inner urge, Druids will go on pilgrimages. This may be as simple as taking a long walk in their local landscape, in a spirit of reverence and 'questing' – seeking solace or inspiration not simply in the attractions of the countryside and the physical exercise, but through the process of walking consciously on the sacred earth.

A pilgrimage might also be more ambitious, journeying perhaps to one of the old places – visiting ancestral lands, travelling to the sourcelands of Druidry, sitting in stone circles, walking the old tracks, allowing oneself to dream, to travel in time and space, and seek new direction not through rational thought, but through moving one's body in space and time, and connecting to sources of power and spiritual nourishment.

A spiritual path also offers the individual seeker a community of fellow-travellers who are inspired by the same ideas and values. In Druidry individuals often gather in groups which are known as groves, just as in Wicca they are known as covens, and in Christianity as congregations. A grove of Druids may number just a few people or several dozen or more. They may meet as often as they wish – usually once a fortnight or so. Together they enact ceremonies, celebrate the festivals, and organize camps or journeys to sacred sites. The Internet enables grove members to keep in touch with each other in their own web-based forums or by email. Some groves are affiliated with particular Druid orders, others are independent with individual members belonging to different orders or none at all. For those orders which offer initiations, groves provide the perfect community to enact such ceremonies.

Each grove will differ in atmosphere, depending upon the people involved, and although they will have their ups and downs, disagreements and schisms, as will any group, often a grove develops a strong sense of tribal loyalty, offering support to members in times of difficulty and providing a deep sense of companionship on the spiritual journey.

Each of the major turning points in life is an initiation in itself and is profoundly significant, physically, psychologically and spiritually. Birth, puberty or coming into adulthood, marriage and death can all be experienced as difficult or traumatic, or as gateways into new realms of experience. Spiritual traditions have always recognized this. One of the problems caused by the increasing secularization of society is that these events are often no longer set within a properly meaningful context, when part of us yearns to honour these special times in a spiritual way.

Druidry offers ceremonies for naming children, weddings and funerals. Some Druids are developing rites for young people to celebrate their transition into adulthood. And rituals are being evolved to mark the time of separation or divorce, helping to release the creative potential of this moment rather than leaving it unmarked, to be remembered only as a time of difficulty or sadness.

EXCERPT FROM A MARRIAGE CEREMONY OF THE ORDER OF BARDS, OVATES AND DRUIDS

Druidess: All things in Nature are circular – night becomes day, day becomes night and night becomes day again. The moon waxes and wanes and waxes again. There is Spring, Summer, Autumn, Winter and then the Spring returns. These things are part of the Great Mysteries.

Michael and Jane, do you bring your symbols of these Great Mysteries of Life?

Jane and Michael: We do.

Druid: Then before all present repeat these words.

Jane (facing Michael and handing him the ring): Accept in freedom this circle of gold as a token of my vows. With it I pledge my love, my strength and my friendship. I bring you joy now and for ever. I vow upon this Holy Earth that through you I honour all men.

Michael (facing Jane and handing her the ring): Accept in freedom this circle of gold as a token of my vows. With it I pledge my love, my strength and my friendship. I bring you joy now and for ever. I vow in the face of Heaven that through you I honour all women.

Jane: In the name of Brighid* I bring you the warmth of my heart (Jane is handed a lighted taper by her mother or female participant).

Michael: In the name of Aengus mac Og* I bring you the light of my love. (Michael is handed a lighted taper by his father or male participant).

They both light a single candle together. (This candle could be kept and relit at each anniversary.)

All: May the warmth and the light of your union be blessed.

Druid: Do you swear upon the Sword of Justice* to keep sacred your vows?

Jane and Michael: We swear.

Druidess: Then seal your promise with a kiss.

Druid: Beneficent Spirits and Souls of our Ancestors, accept the union of your children. Help them, guide them, protect and bless their home and the children born of their union. May their life together reflect the harmony of all life in its perfect union. May they work together in times of ease and times of hardship, knowing that they are truly blessed. From this time forth you walk together along life's path; may your way be blessed.*

*Notes: Brighid is an Irish goddess of healing, smithcraft and poetry, Aengus mac Og is a god of love. Couples may choose different gods or none. The Sword of Justice is a ceremonial sword symbolic of King Arthur's Excalibur. The final blessing comes from a Breton Druid ceremony.

9

Stories and Lore

We have come so far that all the old stories whisper once more.

Robert Duncan

The ritual used in the rites of passage and seasonal ceremonies of Druidry is designed to help participants experience a level of awareness and feeling that is richer than normal. Instead of conveying just intellectual content it uses symbol, metaphor and movement. A psychologist would say that this appeals to the non-dominant hemisphere of the brain that processes art and music as opposed to logic, language and mathematics. A mystic would say that ritual opens us to an experience of the spiritual dimension of life.

In addition to ritual, Druidry makes use of stories, aphorisms and lore to convey much of its essential teachings. The aphorisms tend to follow a three-part pattern and are known as 'Triads'. Many triads were originally used by bards as a mnemonic aid for remembering and composing their poems and stories, but others are clearly designed to stimulate enquiry and offer counsel. In Ireland collections of triads can be found from the ninth century, in Wales from the thirteenth century.

Many are simply lists of threes – the three fairs of Ireland, the three forts of Ireland, the three ardent lovers of the island of Britain, and so on. But every so often, one shines out with its wisdom, displaying an almost oriental simplicity. Here are some examples from early Irish and Welsh triads:

There are three foundations of wisdom: discretion in learning, memory in retaining and eloquence in telling.
Three signs of wisdom: patience, closeness, the gift of prophecy.
Three things hard for a person to do completely: know themselves, conquer their appetite, and keep their secret.
Three counsels of the yellow bird: do not grieve greatly about what has happened, do not believe what cannot be, and do not desire what cannot be obtained.
There are three springs of knowledge: reason, phenomenon and necessity.
The three pillars of achievement: a daring aim; frequent practice; and plenty of failures.

Over the last two hundred years, and as a continuing tradition today, more triads have been created, and it is one of the challenges for students of Druidry to try creating their own.

The animal, plant and tree lore of the Druids has been developed in the modern era from a study of folklore and literature. The Roman writer Pliny wrote that the Druids revered four plants particularly: vervain, selago (an evergreen club moss, probably heath cypress), samolus (probably marshwort) and mistletoe. The Druids told Pliny that vervain should be gathered when Sirius is rising, when neither the sun nor the moon can be seen in the sky. Honey and honeycombs must be offered to the earth, and then the Druid must draw a circle with an iron implement around the plant before pulling it out of the ground with the left hand and raising it in the air. Then the leaves, root and stem should be separated and dried in the shade. Today Druids use vervain as an incense, add it to a bath, place it on an altar or keep it in the bedroom to bring peace and protection to the home. It can also be drunk as a tea to lower fever and to cleanse the kidneys and liver.

Writings on the Ogham tree alphabet of the Druids have helped to build a whole body of lore associated with trees. As an example, the birch tree is known as the 'pioneer tree' since it is often the first tree in the natural creation of a forest. And so it is taken to represent birth, beginnings, newness and the spirit of pioneering. For this reason it is considered auspicious if birch appears in a reading when using Ogham as a method of divination. Appropriately, birch was used to make babies' cradles.

Similarly, a body of animal lore has evolved, based on folk-lore and mythology, and this, too, has been used to create a method of divination (see page 111 for details of animal and tree oracles). As an example, a large amount of folk wisdom has gathered around the bee, to such an extent that an adage found in tales from the Scottish Highlands runs, 'Ask the wild bee what the Druids knew'. Bees are associated with the sun, with mead (used as a sacred drink in Druid rituals) and with the idea of living and working harmoniously together.

The traditional practice of throwing coins in wishing wells can be traced back to the time of the ancient Celts, when wells and springs were considered sacred, and as places to contact the Otherworld. Today people still visit the holy wells of Cornwall and Ireland and throw coins into the wells, saying prayers to St Brighid, the Christianized form of the Celtic goddess Brighid, who is revered by many Druids today.

A medieval tale about sacred wells offers a good example of the way in which modern Druids use old stories to illuminate their understanding of life and feed their desire for mythic nourishment. It is found in 'L'Elucidation', an anonymous prologue to Chrétien de Troyes' twelfth-century 'Conte del Graal'.

The story tells how travellers in Logres, also known as Merlin's Enclosure, or the Isle of Britain, would pause for refreshment beside the old sacred springs and wells that could be found throughout the land. As they tied their horses, or walked weary from their journey to seat themselves beside the water, damsels would appear as if from the Otherworld. Without a word they would serve the travellers with food and drink, drawing water from the wells to pour into golden goblets.

The land flourished as if it were a paradise on earth, until the day black clouds gathered angrily in the sky and violent winds tore the leaves and branches from the trees. It was then that King Amangons arrived at a sacred well. As the damsel of the waters handed him a goblet, filled to the brim with the purest of healing draughts, he looked first at her comely form, and then at the golden vessel. Without a word he decided that both would become his property, and he took hold of the damsel, raping her beside the well, before riding back to his castle with both her and the goblet in his possession.

The knights of Amangons, on seeing the trophies of their king, rode out into the countryside, raping the women of the wells and stealing their vessels wherever they could find them, until none were left to sustain travellers and preserve this ancient tradition. From this moment, the land was struck by drought. It became a wasteland that could only be restored to fertility when the Holy Grail was found. As the original story says: 'The Kingdom was turned to loss, the land was dead and desert as that it was scarce worth a couple of hazel-nuts. For they lost the voices of the wells and the damsels that were therein.'

Although over eight hundred years old, this story speaks to the modern mind with an uncanny urgency, echoing our concerns about the rape of the biosphere and of the resulting wasteland that we are creating around us.

10

Learning Druidry

Training in the bardic tradition is where new seekers begin by learning how to listen and truly hear the voice of the spirit, and so to recover the ancient songs and stories of the ancestors and nature.

Philip Shallcrass and Emma Restall Orr, *A Druid Directory*

Druidry as an Individual Path

Some people attracted to Druidism join a group or order to further their studies or spiritual development. Many more simply begin to adopt Druid beliefs and practices because they find that they reflect feelings and beliefs they already hold about life. When they read or hear about Druidism they experience a sense of familiarity – as if they knew these ideas already, and they just needed to hear them fully articulated from the 'outside' to recognize what they already knew 'inside'.

Druidism places great emphasis on respecting each individual's spiritual integrity, so there are no practices which must be followed in order to be considered a Druid. There is no sense of obligation to celebrate every one of the eight festivals, for example. Being a Druid or following the way of Druidism, is at heart an attitude of mind, broadly based upon the beliefs already outlined, that seeks the development and expression of love, creativity and wisdom. How each person chooses to live from this fundamental attitude towards life is the choice and responsibility of that individual, and no one else. Some choose to treat Druidism as their religion as well as their philosophy of life. Others choose to practise a different religion, such as Christianity, Buddhism or Wicca, while still holding to the core beliefs and principles of Druidism.

Those who follow Druidry without being affiliated with any particular group, usually build their practice and follow their studies through reading books, browsing the Web, and perhaps through attending workshops or retreats, or participating in online discussion forums. While this approach is appealing since it allows flexibility, many people find that they need a more structured approach, or sense the need for some sort of guidance in their spiritual practice and studies. For those people, a number of home-study courses and training programmes now exist. Until 1988 the only way that you could follow a course of study in Druidry, or train in it as a spiritual practice, was to find a teacher to learn directly from. This meant that only a very small number of people followed Druidism. For example I know of only two teachers who were training people in Britain in the 1970s: Ross Nichols and Thomas Maughan.

Today a number of home-study courses exist, and these can be explored through the contacts suggested in the Resources and Contacts section. Discrimination is needed, since nowadays anyone with a home computer can set up a course and offer it on the Internet. The best way to find a course that suits you is to take time to read the introductory material thoroughly. If you are using the internet to research a course, find out about the organization offering it. If they have a message board or Internet forum you could browse that for a while, too, to pick up the atmosphere, although only certain kinds of people use message boards, and on their own they cannot be taken as completely representative of a group. Common sense combined with intuition and discrimination should guide you to the course that is right for you.

The important thing to remember is that following such a course, if it is to be more than simply the intellectual study of a subject, will have an effect on your spiritual and psychological life, so you need to feel comfortable with it, and with being associated with the organization that offers it.

You'll find that most distance-learning teaching is offered not by an individual, but by an 'order'. This helps to avoid a personality cult developing around any particular teacher. The term 'order' is derived from the tradition of magical orders of the nineteenth century,[23] rather than from the idea of Christian religious orders.

The great advantage in taking a home-learning course is that you can choose the depth of engagement that suits you. You may start with a tentative exploration of the subject, then gradually open yourself to a deeper involvement with the exercises and ideas presented, confident in the knowledge that you can set aside such a course at any time.

Distance learning has many advantages: you can follow a course at your own pace, you can study wherever you are in the world, you can work in the quiet and privacy of your own home without having to travel, and now – with the Internet – you can receive the support and advice of fellow students and mentors around the globe. Even so, some people find that in order to learn they need to make contact with other people –

physically, not virtually. They know that they learn best when interacting with others; and there is a tremendous appeal in the idea of finding a spiritual teacher who can directly and personally help us in our quest for wisdom and spiritual development.

Druidry is not a spirituality that is conveyed by 'gurus' who require the devotion of disciples who must accept their every word. Instead it is taught by those who are themselves seekers on a path which is being continually developed. Matt Baker, the founder and head teacher of a school in Arizona that focuses on the creative arts, writes:

> For me the Druid path is a means to create a healthy balanced self in which the higher realizations of spiritual development can be brought down and integrated into the personality. The last forty years of spiritual experimentation in the West has brought many examples of gurus that obviously had some kind of spiritual realization, but whose moral development and character were not of a level that was helpful to their community. Druidry does not produce these kinds of gurus. It produces leaders, artists, healers, and spiritual teachers, who even if they are charismatic in personality, defer to the inner wisdom of the tradition and the inner teacher in their fellow Druids as being the real source of truth. In the end, for me, Druidry has been a practical path that embraces the worldview that life is evolving, the soul is immortal, and we and our fellow creatures are all part of the divine sacred process that is and has been unfolding around us and through us since time began.

Even though Druidry is not taught by 'gurus', people drawn to teaching roles are not immune from the need for attention, approval and affection, and there is always the possibility that a particular teacher's unresolved emotional issues might result in them consciously or unconsciously manipulating or exploiting their students. The familiar way of expressing this idea is to caution that their ego might get in the way of their teaching. From a student's point of view, the only safeguard is their common sense, intuition and ability to be discriminating.

At the present time there are few teachers of Druidism, and the likelihood of finding one close to you may well be remote. If you do come across one, ask them lots of questions: how they trained in Druidism, how long they have been studying, what their aims and intentions are, and more. Listen carefully to their replies and be cautious if you sense pomposity, evasion, fantasy or delusion. A spiritual teacher should display the characteristics of naturalness, humility and humour as well as the qualities of depth, seriousness and integrity.

Rather than finding an individual Druid teacher to learn from, you are more likely to be able to find a group, which is either affiliated to a Druid order or which functions independently. Here you will probably find a strong sense of community, and a group of people who each have something to teach you about Druidism. One or more members of the group may have a strong personality and new members may place them on a pedestal for a while. Over time, though, the star-struck newcomer will usually become aware of the weaknesses as well as the strengths of any dominant personality in the group, and will then come to appreciate that following the Druid path depends upon our becoming more self-reliant rather than less so.

Whether you learn from a course, a teacher or a group, there is one other source of learning that it is vital to draw upon. Druidism is based upon a love of Nature – to such an extent that it is sometimes called a Nature or Earth religion. Druids view Nature as a perpetual source of physical and spiritual nourishment, which can teach us as well as inspire us.

What we learn from the natural world may be intellectual – gained from the observation of animals, plants and the weather for example. Or it may be subtler – the kind of learning that deepens the soul and which cannot be rationally explained, that comes from sleeping out under the stars, meditating in a cave or contemplating a river or the ocean. Both kinds of learning are needed in order to follow the Druid way, and any training in Druidry needs to be firmly grounded within this wider school of experience.

11

The Practical Value of Following Druidism

What attracts people to Druidism is what has attracted people to all forms of mystery schools throughout the ages. It is the search for greater understanding, for deeper experiences, and for communion with the god/dess or Higher Self within. They turn to the nourishment and support of the age-old ways which teach that we are not separate from Nature, but part of it.

Daniel Hansen, *American Druidism*

Orientation and Direction

Life in the modern world can be a confusing experience and there are so many ways in which we can be distracted and disoriented. One of the great advantages of following a spiritual path lies in its ability to offer a sense of orientation and direction. A core belief in Druidry is that we are meant to be on Earth, and that we should focus on being here now, rather than focusing on an 'exit strategy' to escape the illusion of the world, or ensure our place in Heaven. This belief provides us with a strong sense of belonging in the world, and a feeling of participation in life rather than isolation or detachment from it. This orientation opens the way for us to experience the qualities of community, trust, responsibility, empowerment and integrity.

In addition to this purposeful sense of being in the world, Druidry encourages the development of a sense of 'presence', and of being 'grounded' and 'centred' in one's body and in the world. It does this by working with the circle and the directions in ritual and meditation. A circle is cast either physically with a wand or hand, or in the imagination, and then each of the four cardinal directions are faced and greeted. Sometimes a further two directions are acknowledged: above and below. Then the centre is acknowledged. This simple series of actions has the effect of reinforcing our awareness of being in the world, and gives us a strong sense of orientation.

We need to know where we are, but we also need to know where we are going. Druidry aims to provide us with a sense of direction as well as orientation. Its main goals – the cultivation of Wisdom, Love and Creativity – provide Druids with a powerful sense of purpose. Within these broad aims many related goals and directions can be pursued. For example, a Druid working towards the cultivation of their creativity may set their sights on learning to play the harp, or on taking writing classes. Another Druid, working on the cultivation of Love, may decide to focus on developing their love of trees, by spending time in the forest, getting to know and relate to each species there.

Having too many goals can be a distraction in itself, but by offering the three broad goals of Love, Wisdom and Creativity, Druidry aims to give each Druid sufficient direction to generate a sense of purpose, and with this comes enthusiasm, curiosity and a sense of adventure. The myths it uses as source material are steeped in these qualities. The quest for the salmon of wisdom in the old Irish tales, the quest for the three drops of Awen (Inspiration) in the Welsh story of Taliesin, and the quest for the Holy Grail in its many different versions all powerfully evoke the excitement and adventure of the spiritual quest.

In each of these three myths, inspiration is sought – and found. We need inspiration in our lives to help generate a sense of awe and wonder, and to give us ideas and energy. The quest for it is central to Druidry, and in the Tale of Taliesin, it is depicted as an elixir, called Awen. Much of Druid practice is concerned with stimulating the flow of Awen in our lives: the word is chanted or sung in ceremonies to attract inspiration to us, and ritual, meditation and storytelling are all designed to stimulate its flow.

Belief in Awen comes from the understanding that there is more to life than the world of appearances, and that inspiration – ideas, energy, messages – can enter our hearts, minds and bodies from sources beyond us. These sources may emanate from the world of nature, or from other beings – ancestors, nature spirits, spiritual guides, and Deity or deities. Many people, when they experience inspiration, sense it as a flow of energy which is somehow 'impersonal' or 'transpersonal'. They are often astonished at the creative results when they learn how to 'get out of the way' and let this inspiration flow.

In addition to learning how to cultivate Awen, Druids also seek to develop the flow of Nwyfre in their bodies. Nwyfre is the life force that flows through the Universe. Nature is the great source of this energy, and Druids seek to cultivate Nwyfre by spending time outdoors, communing with what they sense as the great primal forces of earth, rain, wind, sun, moon and stars. While Awen brings creative energy and inspiration to our hearts and minds, Nwyfre brings energy and health to our bodies.

However successful we may be in life, and however effective we might be in finding Awen and Nwyfre, events sometimes occur which can leave us in real need of support. A loved one might die or leave us. Illness or some other difficulty might occur, and suddenly all the good health and creative inspiration we may have gathered can seem scattered to the four winds, leaving us bereft and suffering.

A test of the value of a spiritual path lies in the degree to which it is able to offer support in such circumstances. A spirituality needs to offer us a sense of community that we can turn to in times of need, and as Druidry grows in popularity such a community is developing – all over the world. Those lucky enough to have a grove of Druids nearby are able to turn to them for support. Although it is much harder for those who are isolated, the Internet can provide a sense of community, as many of the participants of Druid Internet forums have found.

In addition to a sense of community, we also need wise counsel when we are living through difficult times. This may be provided by fellow Druids, but it can also be found in Druid teachings and writings which have as their aim the fostering of wisdom, love and a creative engagement with life and its difficulties.

When we are going through a difficult time, advice and insight from friends and from books can be a great help. But sometimes nothing they can tell us seems to relieve our suffering. It's as if the crisis is making us turn within – to go deeper than our surface personality to try to find some meaning in our problem. Druids believe that we have a soul, or inner spiritual Self, that is wiser than our everyday personality, and that we can receive guidance from this part of ourselves if we learn how to still the outer mind.

One of the purposes of training in Druidry is to do this: to gain access to sources of support and nourishment for the soul that exist beyond the reach of our everyday personalities – either deep within us or in the Otherworld, where we can receive inspiration, guidance, healing and counsel.

Being of Value to Others and the World

Druidism does not encourage us to focus exclusively on our own spiritual development. Druids care deeply about the state of the world – about the suffering of humans and animals, and of Mother Earth. The belief that many Druids hold in the importance of peace, and in the principle of 'harmlessness', influences their actions profoundly, and most Druids are involved in initiatives to protect the environment. Some may simply contribute to Greenpeace or Friends of the Earth. Others may be more actively involved in trying to protect certain species or habitats. Most will support tree-planting and refor-estation projects, and the maxim 'think globally, act locally' has been taken to heart by many Druids, who are involved in local community initiatives to protect and improve the environment.

12

Druidry in the Future

The approaching transformation requires people, groups, and communities to be ready to preserve legacies for the future, so that as the vast tottering structure of industrial civilization comes apart, seeds can be planted that will bear fruit in times to come. I suggest that the Druid community prepare itself to fill that role, and to save and plant those seeds.

John Michael Greer, *Druidry and the Future* [24]

Towards the end of the twentieth century Druidism moved out of the shadows of obscurity, and began to take its place amongst the ranks of seriously considered spiritual traditions. Until then it had existed on the margins of acceptance because there was a lack of understanding of its history, identity and potential value.

Critics argued that it was an invented tradition since an unbridgeable chasm of over a thousand years separated ancient Druids from the Revival Druids of the seventeenth and later centuries. Iolo Morganwg had fabricated most of the material used by the fraternal and cultural Druids, and those who were trying to practise a Druidism that offered a path of spiritual development were in reality simply combining the work of Iolo with material from a variety of world religions and esoteric traditions. But from the 1960s Druids began turning to different sources of inspiration – in particular Celtic studies and archetypal psychology. Some, especially in America, have rejected the previous few centuries of Revivalism as aberrant and have tried to create a Druidism based solely upon historical authenticity. Others, mostly in Britain, have attempted to incorporate new material, while retaining elements of the Druid Revival that they feel are effective, arguing that many spiritual traditions and varieties of religion are of recent origin, and were introduced with 'creation myths' that were less than accurate historically.[25]

By doing this, a process of reclaiming history has begun which is set to accelerate in the coming years. As Revival Druidry is explored, rather than weakening its claim to be authentic, Druidism is likely to develop an even stronger sense of tradition and pride in its heritage. This will undoubtedly be helped by a major five-year study of the last three hundred years of Druidism, due for completion in 2008, funded by the government's Arts and Humanities Research Board, which is being carried out by the history department of Bristol University.

This process of strengthening a sense of tradition is likely to continue in another area which has attracted criticism in the past: the association between modern-day Druids and stone circles. Although there is no historical evidence that the Druids built megalithic monuments, the fact is that modern Druids love stone circles and like to perform ceremonies in them. For the last two hundred years they have been creating them and celebrating in them. In Wales stone circles are often built for the Eisteddfod celebrations, and one of the most well-known examples of a modern circle stands in a field used each year for the

Glastonbury music festival. Though some Druids (and their critics) continue to deny the validity of this by-now traditional activity, most enjoy it.

It is also possible that the future may prove that their spiritual forebears did indeed build circles, since some academics are now pointing to a new sense of continuity in the genetics and culture of the British, with the rejection of the idea of a Celtic 'invasion' that introduced Druidism a thousand years after the last circles had been built. This school of thought makes it possible to see the Druids as the priests and priestesses of these ancient monuments, a tendency reinforced by the increasing recognition of the importance of ritual astronomy in their construction.

Recently, Professor Ronald Hutton has written:

> In building their case against modern Druidry, [the archaeologists] Kendrick, Piggott, Atkinson and Daniel all made great play with the fact that ancient Druids could no longer be definitely credited either with building the monument or with officiating within it. They were, however, scrupulous enough to recognise two difficulties. The first is that prehistorians have so far been unable to determine how far continuities of religious tradition and practice did or did not exist through the periods between the Neolithic and the Iron Age. The second is that there is some evidence for activity in and around Stonehenge during the Iron Age itself. It may be that, whether or not modern Druids ever make a significant reappearance at the monument, ancient Druids could yet be fated to do so.[26]

Research into the recent history of Druidry is likely to shed further light on many of the outstanding figures in the Druid movement over the last three hundred years who have been political radicals and non-conformists. As the environmental and economic challenges that face the world become increasingly urgent, we need spiritual approaches that encourage a social conscience and the audacity to think radically. With its history of thinkers who have championed social and economic justice it is not surprising that Druidry today attracts environmental activists and social reformers, and this trend is likely to continue. Author Brendan Myers focuses on the value of Druidry in his *Dangerous Religion – Environmental Spirituality and Its Activist Dimension*, John Michael Greer, Chief of the *Ancient Order of Druids in America*, has begun to speak openly about the serious difficulties the world will face when the supply of oil runs out,[27] and anti-globalization campaigners draw inspiration from a spiritual tradition that has championed radical approaches to injustice – from the days when Druid leaders supported the Chartists to modern times when Druids support environmental and road-protest campaigns.

Druidry's radical stance extends to the politics of the body and sexuality. For at least three generations significant Druid leaders in England have supported the cause of Naturism – believing that nudism can bring one into closer contact with Nature.[28] More recently, in America, some Druids have pointed to the ancient Celts' acceptance of multiple sexual relationships to advocate the practice of 'polyamory'.[29] Not all Druids would accept that being naked or non-monogamous is connected with Druidism, but a liberal and tolerant spirit characterizes the modern Druid, and it is unlikely that they would be upset by the practice of either activity amongst consenting adults.

Despite the generally tolerant atmosphere in which most Druidry is conducted, there can be strong differences of opinion – expressed either through Internet message boards or in discussion. Those who treat Druidry as a neo-Pagan religion can find it hard to understand how anyone can follow both Druidism and Christianity. Those who reject the contributions of Revival Druidism and strive towards an approach which is called 'Celtic Reconstructionism' can be baffled as to why someone might want to recite a prayer that was most likely fabricated in the eighteenth century. Those who find no need to include concepts of deity or deities in their spiritual life can find it hard to empathize with the approach of a Druid who performs devotionals to specific deities. Some Druids are attracted to the idea of Druidism as a Universalist philosophy that sees the commonalities in all faiths, while others find this alien, and seek instead to practise Druidry as a magical craft or philosophy which is specific rather than universal.

Druids in Britain view with bemusement American attempts to construct a religion that bases itself on a church model, complete with legal registration as a church, pages of by-laws and clergy-training programmes, since part of Druidry's appeal for them lies in its dissimilarity to the church, and its avoidance of regulations and distinctions between clergy and laity. Some Americans in their turn find British Druidry oddly unstructured and laissez-faire.

For the most part each different approach to Druidry simply goes about its business without paying too much attention to the other approaches. Fraternal and cultural druids exist in separate worlds, and the Celtic Reconstructionist and American religious groups generally ignore the majority of British publications and groups and vice versa, perhaps out of tacit disapproval of each other's approaches, perhaps because they are just busy enough as it is. An interesting project for the future would be to bring together these different viewpoints to explore their commonalities and differences.

There are strong precedents for such a project. Over the last fifteen years a number of dialogues have been initiated to explore common ground and misconceptions. The widespread belief that Druidism is patriarchal or suitable only for men has been substantially eroded thanks to women's involvement in Druidry. Women now lead groups, write books on feminine perspectives in the tradition, and form over half the membership of most Druid groups. Until recently both Christians and Wiccans often felt that Druidry was alien to them. But a number of Christian and Druid conferences hosted by an Anglican and a Catholic priest in the early 1990s, and a Christian, Wiccan and Druid conference held in 1996 has helped to build bridges. A type of practice, termed DruidCraft, that combines Druidry and Wicca (also known as 'the Craft') has evolved, and Christians who also follow Druidism as a spiritual path have begun to speak up – writing articles and creating webpages.[30]

Druidry's strength lies in its inclusivity and its tolerance of diversity. Just as Nature is generous and biodiversity is a sign of health, so in the worlds of culture and spirituality differences of opinion create a healthy and exotic environment, with the potential for the cross-fertilization of ideas. Druidry is not simply Paganism, or religion or philosophy – it can be each of these things and others besides.

Not everything in the world of Druidry is rosy, however. One can find a streak of racism in certain minor and dwindling expressions of the tradition. These suggest that only 'Celts' can genuinely follow the way of the Druid, and in France have become associated with nationalist movements and right-wing politics. Such approaches ignore the latest researches in genetics and culture which show that Celticism is a cultural and not a racial definition, and ignore too the fact that although Druidry originally emerged out of a tribal context in the lands we now consider Celtic, its revival in the modern era has allowed it to spread and flower in a way that makes it accessible to all people regardless of their cultural or ethnic origins. Unlike Native American or Australian aboriginal traditions which are practised by indigenous cultures, Druidry has evolved as a spiritual project of the western European imagination that bases itself on Celtic mythology and lore, but it is not a tribal practice that has been handed down through the generations. What it loses in romantic appeal because of this, it gains in its universal appeal and relevance to the contemporary situation. It is simply misguided and selfish to attempt to confine its practice to one type of person.

Another unattractive side of Druidism can be found in some truly awful books that have been published in the last few years. These range from a misogynistic fantasy that pretends to convey ancient knowledge, to a titillating manual on group 'sex magic' written by someone who claims descent from a lineage of Welsh Druids.

Bad books and racists are thankfully in the minority. In the last fifteen years the quantity of publications on Druidry has soared. Prior to 1990 the problem was finding a single book or article on the subject. Now the problem lies in choosing which one to read. There are in-house journals of Druid groups in English, Dutch and French and *The Druids' Voice* magazine, published by the British Druid Order, has a broad public readership.

The rapid growth of Druidism in the last few decades is likely to continue as the environmental crisis deepens, as church attendances decline and as alternative approaches to spirituality receive more attention. Most Druidry is conveyed through the structure of 'orders' – groups that see themselves as Mystery Schools or teaching organizations. This type of structure has benefited thousands of spiritual seekers over the years, but it has also limited Druidry's appeal. Many people want to practise a Nature spirituality without the restrictions they feel such a structure implies. An 'order' seems to them old-fashioned, with religious overtones. Even though many orders are far from being old-fashioned and instead encourage non-conformity and eccentricity, by their very nature they require a commitment and a desire to join a group that many people do not have. Just as orders have their place in a number of traditions – including the Christian, Buddhist and Sufi – so they will undoubtedly continue to exist in Druidism. But Druidry's greatest challenge in the future will be to find ways of expression that offer an alternative to this traditional structure. Attempts to create this have already begun: the Druid Network was launched in 2003 to provide a new way of presenting and uniting Druids, relying solely on the Internet. And in 2005 the Avalon College of Druidry was founded in the USA with the intention of creating a university specializing in Druid studies.

It may well be the next generation that evolves other forms that speak to the needs of an ever-widening circle of spiritual seekers. Certainly the next generation will see the first substantial amount of people in modern times attaining adulthood who have been raised with Druid values, beliefs and practices. They will have inherited a spiritual path ideally suited to the era they will be living in: an environmental spirituality that cherishes all life on Earth, and that seeks to preserve and protect it for the benefit of all beings.

Notes

1 Personal communication. International Grand Lodge of Druidism, July 2005.

2 Hutton, Ronald. '*Witches, Druids and King Arthur*', Hambledon & London, 2003, p. 258.

3 'American Religious Identification Survey', by the Graduate Center of the City University of New York, at http://www.gc.cuny.edu

4 In 2002 the UK's Pagan Federation estimated the number of UK Pagans to be between 50,000 and 200,000. 38,000 people declared themselves as Pagan in the 2001 Census of Population, making it the eighth most popular faith in Britain.

5 Bonewits, Isaac, *The Pagan Man: Priests, Warriors, Hunters, and Drummers*, Citadel Press, 2005, p. 11.

6 Email to author, April 2005.

7 Caesar, Julius, *De Bello Gallico*, VI,13–18.

8 Nichols, Ross, *The Book of Druidry: History, Sites and Wisdom*, Thorsons, 1990.

9 Although the majority of cultural and fraternal Druidry was practised by the Welsh and English respectively, cultural Druidism did spread in the early twentieth century to Brittany and Cornwall, and fraternal Druidry worldwide.

10 The process of becoming interested in Celtic sources began under the chieftainship of Robert MacGregor Reid, but Ross Nichols intensified and developed it.

11 Prescott, Andrew. 'The Voice Conventional': Druidic Myths and Freemasonry, http://www.shef.ac.uk/~crf/papers/druid.htm.

12 Australia, Denmark, Finland, Germany, Iceland, Norway, the Netherlands, New Zealand, Surinam, Sweden, Switzerland, the UK and the USA.

13 Though cultural Druids were considerably embarrassed when, in the 1950s, Dr G. J. Williams provided conclusive evidence of Iolo's fraud.

14 As an example, Charles Graves, the grandfather of Robert Graves whose book *The White Goddess* was seminal in the revival of interest in Goddess worship and Paganism, was an expert on the Ogham tree alphabet, and on early Irish law. He initiated a Royal Commission to transcribe and translate this treasure trove of information, which was published in six volumes between 1865 and 1901.

15 Berresford Ellis, Peter, *The Druids*, Constable, 1994, pp. 96–7.

16 Kinsella, Thomas, *The Tain*, Dolmen Press, Dublin, 1969.

17 Email to author from Prof. Ronald Hutton, 28 September 2004.

18 See, for example, Michael Newton, *Journey of Souls: Case Studies of Life Between Lives*, Llewellyn, 1994.

19 Gardner, Gerald, *The Meaning of Witchcraft*, Aquarian Press, 1959.

20 *Geographica*, IV, 4, 197–8 (trans. W. Dinan, quoted in John Matthews (ed.), *The Druid Source Book*, Blandford, 1997, p. 18).

21 Myers, Brendan, *Dangerous Religion: Environmental Spirituality and Its Activist Dimension*, Earth Religions Press, 2003.

22 Excerpted and adapted from Internet article 'The Brehon Laws: Defining Ethics and Values for Modern Druidry', by Athelia Nihtscada, at www.druidnetwork.org

23 Starting with 'The Hermetic Order of the Golden Dawn'.

24 From an Internet article at http://www.aoda.org/articles/Druidry.htm.

25 Examples of movements whose origin myths have been proved historically inaccurate, and whose practices and teachings have been created within the last two hundred years include Mormonism, Theosophy, Rosicrucianism and Wicca.

26 From the journal *British Archaeology*, Summer 2005.

27 See *Druidry and the Future – An Open Letter to the Druid Community* by John Michael Greer on www.aoda.org/articles/Druidry.htm.

28 See the essay 'Clothed with the Sky – A Spiritual Form of Naturism within Druidry' at http://www.druidry.org, 'The Druid Tradition', under 'Naturism', 'Skyclad Druidry'.

29 Ellison, Robert, *The Solitary Druid*, Citadel Press, 2005.

30 See the section entitled 'Christians & Druids' under 'The Druid Tradition' at www.druidry.org.

Glossary

Alban Arthan – the Druid festival of the Winter Solstice, loosely translated as 'The Light of Arthur'.

Alban Eilir – the Druid festival of the Spring Equinox, loosely translated as 'The Light of the Earth'.

Alban Elfed – the Druid festival of the Autumn Equinox, loosely translated as 'The Light of Water'.

Alban Hefin – the Druid festival of the Summer Solstice, loosely translated as 'The Light of the Shore'.

Awen (Welsh) – inspiration, the gift or blessing of the gods generally, or the Goddess Ceridwen, Patroness of the Bards, specifically. Equivalent to *Imbas* (Irish).

Bard – in ancient times, a poet and storyteller who trained in a Bardic college. In modern times, one who sees their creativity as an innate spiritual ability, and who chooses to nurture that ability partly or wholly with Druidism.

Beltane/Bealteinne – the Druid festival dedicated to celebrating Spring and the union of God and Goddess. Meaning 'The Good Fire', Beltane celebrations usually include leaping over a bonfire. Celebrated around 1 May in the northern hemisphere, 1 October in the southern.

Druid – in ancient times a philosopher, teacher, counsellor and magician, the word probably meaning 'A Forest Sage' or 'Strong Seer'. In modern times, one who follows Druidry as their chosen spiritual path, or who has entered the Druid level of training in a Druid Order.

DruidCraft – a type of spiritual practice that combines Druidry with the 'Craft' of Wicca, or when written with a small 'c' can refer to the 'craft' of Druidry.

Eisteddfod (plural Eisteddfodau) – a Bardic festival and competition of the performing arts, from the Welsh, meaning 'a session or assembly'. Usually opened with a Druid ceremony.

Equinox – the times in Spring and Autumn when day and night are of equal duration. They represent times of balance and also turning points of the year as the seasons change, and are celebrated in Druidry with ceremonies.

Gorsedd (plural Gorseddau) – a term used in Welsh Druidry to describe an Assembly or group of Druids. The term means literally 'high seat', and originally referred to prehistoric sacred mounds, which were used as places of assembly for the inauguration of kings, law-giving and festival celebration. A Druid Gorsedd usually opens an Eisteddfod.

Imbolc/Oimelc – the Druid festival of the Goddess, particularly Brighid, celebrated around 1 February in the northern hemisphere, 1 August in the southern.

Lughnasadh/Lammas – the Druid festival of the Harvest, celebrated around 1 August in the northern hemisphere, 1 February in the southern.

Nwyfre – the Druid term for 'Life force', probably derived from an ancient Celtic word 'Naomh' – firmament.

Otherworld – the world or reality that exists in parallel with the physical/everyday world, that we visit sometimes in dreams or meditation, and that Druids believe we travel to on the death of the physical body.

Ovate – in ancient times a prophet, seer, healer and diviner. In modern times, one who studies or practises herbalism, healing and divination within a Druidic context, or who has entered the Ovate level of training within a Druid Order.

Revival Druidry or 'The Revival Period' – the time during the seventeenth to nineteenth centuries when Druidism was rediscovered and reinvented.

Samhuinn/Samhain – the Druid festival of the Ancestors – a time for honouring those who have died, celebrated around 1 November in the northern hemisphere, 1 May in the southern.

Solstice – the time in Summer when the day is longest, and in Winter when the day is shortest. They represent times of powerful celestial and terrestrial influence, and are celebrated in Druidry with ceremonies.

Further Reading

For introductory books on Druidism as a spiritual path, see *Druid Mysteries, Ancient Wisdom for the 21st Century* by Philip Carr-Gomm, Rider, 2002; *A Guide to Druidry* by Philip Shallcrass, Piatkus, 2000; *Druids – A Beginner's Guide* by Cairistiona Worthington, Hodder, 1999, and *Principles of Druidry* by Emma Restall Orr, Thorsons, 1998. Each book is short and easy to read, and includes practical exercises. Although they are introductory, they are written by people with years of experience in Druidry, and each one contributes something unique to an understanding of what Druidism is, and how it can help you.

For an illustrated history that includes the modern period, see *Exploring the World of the Druids* by Dr Miranda J. Green, Thames & Hudson, 1998. For a history of ancient Druidry, see *The Druids* by Peter Berresford Ellis, Constable, 1994 and *The Druids – Celtic Priests of Nature* by Jean Markale, Inner Traditions, 1999.

For an inspirational book that draws on Druidic and Celtic sources:
The Celtic Spirit – Daily Meditations for the Turning Year by Caitlin Matthews, Harper SanFrancisco, 1999. Quotations, questions, essays and meditations.
Kindling the Celtic Spirit by Mara Freeman, HarperSanFrancisco, 2001. Teachings, poetry, recipes, stories and folklore related to each of the seasons.

To explore aspects of Druidry in depth see:
The Druidry Handbook by John Michael Greer, Weiser, 2006.
Living Druidry by Emma Restall Orr, Piatkus, 2004.
The Bardic Source Book ed. by John Matthews, Blandford, 1998.
The Celtic Seers' Source Book ed. by John Matthews, Cassell, 1999.
The Druid Source Book ed. by John Matthews, Blandford, 1996.
The Encyclopaedia of Celtic Wisdom ed. by John and Caitlin Matthews, Rider, 2001.
The Making of a Druid: Hidden Teachings from the Colloquy of Two Sages by Christian J. Guyonvarc, Inner Traditions, 2002.

To explore the work of a key figure in modern Druidry, Ross Nichols, a biography, photos, and selections of his paintings and poetry can be seen at www.druidry.org. Also see:

The Book of Druidry by Ross Nichols, Thorsons, 1990.
In the Grove of the Druids – the Druid Teachings of Ross Nichols by Philip Carr-Gomm, Watkins, 2002.
Journeys of the Soul – The Life and Legacy of a Druid Chief by Philip Carr-Gomm with the Letters and Travel Diaries of Ross Nichols, Thoth, 2007.

To explore the shamanic aspects of Druidry see *Fire in the Head – Shamanism and the Celtic Spirit* by Tom Cowan, HarperSanFrancisco, 1993.

To explore the relationship between Druidry and Wicca see *Druidcraft – The Magic of Wicca and Druidry* by Philip Carr-Gomm, Thorsons, 2002.

To learn how a Druidic understanding can be used when exploring the landscape see *The Druid Way* by Philip Carr-Gomm, Thoth, 2006.

To read a wide range of contributions from Druids around the world, which include essays on history, healing, ritual, herbs, star-lore and more, see *The Rebirth of Druidry*, edited by Philip Carr-Gomm, Thorsons, 2003.

To explore the Feminine perspective in Druidry, see:
Druid Priestess by Emma Restall Orr, Thorsons, 2001.
The Modern-Day Druidess by Cassandra Eason, Piatkus, 2003.
A Druid Abroad – A Quest for the Lady in Druidry by Sandra Parsons, Capall Bann, 2003.

To explore Druid oracles, see:
The Druid Arrival Oracle by Philip and Stephanie Carr-Gomm, Connections, 1994.
The DruidCraft Tarot, by Philip and Stephanie Carr-Gomm, Connections, 2004.
The Celtic Tree Oracle by Liz and Col Murray, Rider, 1989.

Resources and Contacts

The Internet

To learn more about Druidry, the Internet is a powerful resource. Just type 'Druidry' or 'Druid' into a search engine and a wealth of sites will be offered. An excellent guide is The Druid Network's website at www.druidnetwork.org, which offers profiles of most Druid organisations, book reviews, events listings and more. Another major resource is the Order of Bards, Ovates and Druids website at www.druidry.org, which has over two thousand pages of information, including a library, sections on training in Druidry, Druid camps, the Sacred Grove Planting Programme, the Campaign for Ecological Responsibility, a bookshop, and comprehensive links to many other sites. The Message Board has over 2,000 members and represents the largest Druid community on the Internet.

Courses and Groups

The Order of Bards, Ovates & Druids offers an experience-based home-learning course that guides you through the three grades of Bard, Ovate and Druid. Each month teaching material is mailed to you, and you have the support of a mentor to whom you can write or email. In addition there are workshops, camps and celebrations in Britain and the USA and other parts of the world, and over eighty groves and seed-groups where you can meet and work with other members. The course is also available in an audio version and in French, German and Dutch. Full details from: OBOD, PO Box 1333, Lewes, East Sussex, BN7 1DX. Tel/fax +44 (0)1273 470888. Email OBOD@druidry.org or see www.druidry.org.

The British Druid Order runs camps and workshops, organizes festivals and celebrations and publishes books and magazines: BDO, PO Box 635, Halifax, HX2 6WX, UK, www.druidorder.demon.co.uk.

In the USA the three main Druid groups are the Ancient Order of Druids in America, PO Box 1181, Ashland, OR 97520, www.aoda.org; The Henge of Keltria, PO Box 4305, Clarksburg, WV 26302, www.keltria.org; and ADF, 859 N. Hollywood Way, Box 368, Burbank, CA 91505, www.adf.org.

Information on most of the other Druid organizations can be found on www.druidnetwork.org and in *A Druid Directory* by Philip Shallcrass and Emma Restall Orr, published by the BDO. Copies are available from the BDO and from the OBOD online bookshop.

Index

Keep in touch with
Granta Books:

Visit granta.com to discover more.

GRANTA